THE FIRE STILL
burns

THE FIRE STILL
burns

LIFE IN

PURICH
BOOKS

SAM
GEORGE

with JILL YONIT GOLDBERG *and* LIAM BELSON,
DYLAN MacPHEE, *and* TANIS WILSON

Purich Books, an imprint of UBC Press
2029 West Mall
Vancouver, BC, V6T 1Z2
www.purichbooks.ca

32 31 30 29 28 27 26 25 24 23   5 4 3 2 1

Printed in Canada on FSC-certified ancient-forest-free paper
(100% post-consumer recycled) that is processed
chlorine- and acid-free.

LIBRARY AND ARCHIVES CANADA CATALOGUING IN PUBLICATION

Title: The fire still burns : life in and after residential school /
Sam George with Jill Yonit Goldberg and Liam Belson,
Dylan MacPhee, and Tanis Wilson.

Names: George, Sam (Samuel James), author. |
Goldberg, Jill Yonit, author. | Belson, Liam, author. |
MacPhee, Dylan, author. | Wilson, Tanis, author.

Identifiers:
Canadiana (print) 2023015929X | Canadiana (ebook) 2023016126X |
ISBN 9780774880855 (softcover) | ISBN 9780774880862 (PDF) |
ISBN 9780774880879 (EPUB)

Subjects: LCSH: George, Sam (Samuel James) | LCSH: St. Paul's
Residential School (Squamish) | CSH: First Nations—British
Columbia—Residential schools. | CSH: First Nations—Education
—British Columbia. | CSH: First Nations children—Crimes against. |
CSH: First Nations children—Violence against. |
CSH: First Nations—Biography. | LCGFT: Autobiographies.

Classification: LCC E96.6.S173 G46 2023 | DDC 371.829/9794—dc23

UBC Press gratefully acknowledges the financial support for
our publishing program of the Government of Canada, the Canada
Council for the Arts, and the British Columbia Arts Council.

Frontispiece image:
St. Paul's Indian Residential School class photo with a young
Sam George sitting on the newel post at the foot of the stairs, c. 1952.
Located in North Vancouver, St. Paul's began operations in 1899
and closed on September 1, 1959.
Archives Deschâtelets-NDC, n.d., 10a-c000786-d0002-001

For all those who didn't make it

CONTENTS

PREFACE

MY NAME IS Sam George. In spite of everything that happened to me, by the grace of the Creator I have lived to be an Elder.

St. Paul's Indian Residential School tried to take everything from me. The schools tried to chase away the Indianness from all of us who went to them. They tried to change our thoughts and the way we acted.

I am one of the lucky ones who survived. They beat me and punished me, and, like everyone, I complied, behaving how they wanted me to, doing what the nuns and priests asked. I survived because my culture and my identity were deep within me, and they couldn't touch that. My culture brought me back to myself.

I'm still here.

I tell my story so that people like me will know they're not alone and might find comfort in knowing that.

I also tell my story so that the younger generation will learn from it and will make sure that nothing like residential school ever happens again.

– SAM GEORGE

ACKNOWLEDGMENTS

BIG HYCHKA TO Tanis Wilson, Dylan MacPhee, and Liam Belson for your work on this memoir. Hychka to my big friend Jill Goldberg for all the writing and editing, and for encouraging me all the way. Hychka to Nadine Pedersen for your guidance, and extra special hychka to Michelle LaBoucane for your love and support.

– SAM GEORGE

THANK YOU AND much respect to Liam Belson, Dylan MacPhee, and Tanis Wilson for your beautiful work, which evolved into *The Fire Still Burns*. Thank you to Rick Ouellet for your guidance and wisdom, which shaped Writing Lives and the connections that have been necessary for it to run. Thank you to the Indian Residential School Survivors Society, especially Angela White and Wesley Scott, for partnering with the Writing Lives course. Much gratitude to Rachel Mines for providing the template for the course. Tremendous thanks to the team at Purich Books, especially Nadine Pedersen and Michelle van der Merwe, for all your editorial guidance, patience, and devotion to this book. And, of course, my most heartfelt thanks of all to Sam George for letting me into your life and permitting me to hear your story, and to Michelle LaBoucane for welcoming me with such warmth and kindness – hychka!

– JILL YONIT GOLDBERG

A NOTE ON THE TEXT

THIS BOOK IS A work of nonfiction. Certain names have been omitted from the text, and care has been taken not to tell the stories of anyone other than Sam George. In the course of telling Sam's story, it is inevitable that other people's lives are described in a limited fashion, and others may remember things differently; however, these are Sam's memories of events.

This book portrays instances of racism, cultural abuse, child abuse, emotional abuse, sexual abuse, domestic abuse, assault, drug and alcohol use and withdrawal, mention of suicide, and other content that some may find disturbing. Readers who have experienced similar trauma are encouraged to have a self-care plan in place, to remember their strengths, and to seek help if needed.

Phonetic spellings have been provided in footnotes, where applicable.

....

> *For more on the writing process and how this book came to be, please see the Afterword. And for information related to residential schools, trauma, the Truth and Reconciliation Commission of Canada, and crisis support resources, please refer to the Reader's Guide.*

THE FIRE STILL
burns

1

Your Name Is Tseatsultux

WHEN WE WERE growing up, my Ta'ah (grandmother), my Papa (grandfather), and other Elders taught us the history of our Sḵwx̱wú7mesh (Squamish) People. They were always telling stories to the younger generations. We have had three Hereditary Chiefs in our family, which is pretty big business. My grandfather George Johnny was Chief of the former False Creek Reserve, which was located in an area of Vancouver now known as Kitsilano. He was a brother of Chief Khatsahlano. Another one of my Ancestors was a Chief back in Upper Squamish, which is the whole area around where the town of Squamish is today.

Right where Kitsilano is, right where the Burrard Street Bridge is, the settlers forced my people to leave their Traditional Territory because they were going to occupy the land. My people also had Traditional Territory in what is now called New Westminster. At Kitsilano, they put my people on a barge, floated them out into the deep waters, then cut them loose. The settlers made them drift for a long time, until they came across some paddlers who helped them reach safety. My great-grandfather and my grandfather were part of that group stranded on the barge. My great-great-great-grandfather had offered to buy the land from the settlers but was denied. Indians weren't allowed to buy land. So, the story goes, the settlers forced the Squamish People onto a boat and drifted them away from their own land.

My name is Sam, Samuel George. I was born in June 1944 and have lived most of my life on Eslhá7an.[1] Our reserve is located in North Vancouver, by the water, and when I think about home, this is what I think of. I was born and raised there. The colonized name is Mission Reserve because it has a church on it. I was named after my uncle, who was overseas fighting in the Second World War; he was my mother's brother. There was about a two-year difference between each of my siblings and me. My brother Ross, who has passed on, was the oldest, then Margaret, who is about four years older than me. Next is Andy, who is two years older than I am, then me and my baby sister, Beatrice, or Honey Bee. I don't know – nobody seems to know – but I think it was one of our aunts who called her Honey Bee. We were all very close in early life. We took care of each other. When Mom had to go to Vancouver, Dad was working, or our parents were gone all day, Ross and Margaret would cook for us. They'd make sandwiches for us younger kids. Andy took especially good care of me.

Ross was really level-headed and protective. He always reminded us that if we were in trouble, or if we needed help, to get him. I only have one memory of him getting mad at me. Margaret was more the motherly type. She was constantly caring for us. My brother Andy and I were close. Whatever he was doing, I was right there with him. Beatrice, my baby sister, was my agitator, I guess. We became good friends. We would go to the movies or just do stuff together, until I got mixed up with all the guys. When I started

. . . .

1 Pronounced *[Ut-sla-han]*.

going with the guys, I'd get mad at her when she tried to tag along.

Dad – Stephen, or Flossie they called him – was a long-shoreman, a hunter and fisherman too. My dad's nickname was Flossie because he had a girlfriend when he was really young, and her name was Flossie. He had five brothers, so they gave him the nickname. For the rest of his life, everyone called him Flossie. My dad was quite a bit older than my mom. I think he had about twenty years on her. I know he was born in the early 1900s. I know this because he was too young for the First World War, but too old for the Second World War. My mom's name was Josephine, and my Ta'ah's English name was Margaret. She was born in the 1800s and got married when she was only twelve. She had sixteen children, though they didn't all survive. My Papa was tall – at least six feet. I don't remember his traditional name, but we just called him Papa. His English name was Willie. They didn't call each other that, though. They had their traditional names, and I remember them calling each other by their traditional names. My traditional name is Tseatsultux,[2] and it goes back five generations that we know of. It was my dad's grandfather's (also named George Johnny) traditional name. My Ta'ah told me, "Your name is Tseatsultux," and she made me repeat it about four or five times to remember it.

I always had a crewcut back then. My hair was always cut short. My brother Ross was like that too. It was the fashion in them days. Whenever he went for a haircut, he'd bring me. I usually wore hand-me-down clothes as well. I got Andy's clothes. If I got anything new, it would be shoes or socks, but the other clothes were hand-me-downs.

....

2 *Pronounced [Tse-at-sul-tux].*

Dad was quite short. He got my Ta'ah's height, that's for sure. He was sort of a tough guy. We always viewed him that way. He used to be a boxer. He also had short black hair, and he combed it straight back every morning, and he had a really thick beard. He'd shave once in the morning and then once more before he went to bed. He dressed like a long-shoreman – you know, jeans, workboots, and a jacket with a hat. My mom was heavy, and she liked to dress up. She liked to put makeup on and do her hair. Mom had long silky hair, but she didn't go to the hairdresser or anything. Her sisters or cousins would visit, and they would do each other's hair and share makeup.

My oldest memory is of my first Christmas tree, from when I was quite young, at just over a year old. I know this because I could hardly walk, and back then Margaret packed me around a lot. We had a wood stove, and my mom put us kids around it, and my dad filled it up with wood to make sure we were kept warm all night. We lived in a very old house and it smelled like old wood. It had old wooden floors, old paint, and sometimes you could smell the windows. They were just single-pane, so the house was either too hot or too cold. My siblings and I used to sleep around the wood stove, but once my parents built the upstairs, it became our bed-room. It was one open room, which was the whole length of the upstairs.

I guess while we were all sleeping, Mom and Dad brought the Christmas tree, decorated it, and lit it up. I remember waking up one morning to really excited voices. I remember crawling on my bed, looking over, and there was this beauti-ful tree. I didn't understand the meaning yet, but I remember looking at it, just staring at it. When Margaret glanced over, she saw me kneeling on the bed and she came running over, picked me up, and carried me over to the tree. She sat me down in front of it, and I remember looking at it in awe. It was sparkling, bubbling, and flashing off and on. In them days, they would decorate it with candy. Little strings of candy went from the top to the bottom. I remember my sister breaking off some candy and putting it in my mouth. That's my first recollection of sweets.

Suppertime was a big time. While Dad was working, I remember my grandmother, his mother, coming over with my Papa. All the women would be sitting at the table chopping up the meat and the veggies, or potatoes, or making the rice. While they were getting the supper ready, they would all be talking. Maybe three or four of them, not a whole bunch, but the thing about them talking was that they were speaking the Squamish language. My parents mostly spoke to us in English but they were fluent in Squamish, and all of the adults, including our grandparents, spoke to each other in it. Growing up, there was a mixture of English and Squamish spoken in our house. In them days I could understand the Squamish language, though I couldn't speak it fluently because I was too young. We would just listen whenever the adults were speaking among themselves. You know, my grandparents, my Papa and Ta'ah, barely spoke English. They spoke broken English, but they used to talk to us in Squamish. They would mostly say stuff like, "Be careful. Watch out. Don't do that." I can still understand some words.

When the women were cooking, my Papa would be outside chopping away and keeping the cookstove burning. I remember going out there with him, thinking I was helping, but he'd be telling me, "Watch your fingers. Keep your fingers away." He'd be chopping wood, then we'd load it all up and he'd give me one piece. We'd both walk in and keep the fire going. Finally, when the supper came, my dad would arrive home from work and we'd all run to meet him. I would be going for his hand to hold, and my older siblings went for his lunch bucket. When they opened up his lunch bucket, there were always cookies or fruit in there: an apple, orange, or whatever. He would always have enough for us, you know – just part of the game he played, I guess. After that, we'd all sit down for supper. Everyone would be around the table talking, gossiping, joking, teasing – and all in the Squamish language. When we finished eating, the grandmothers and the women would clean the dishes, and Dad and Papa would go sit in the living room and just talk. Sometimes Ross would sit with them too.

Back then, my Ta'ah was the most important person to me. Ta'ah was very short – probably not even five feet, and heavy. I remember she smelled either like soap from cleaning or like frybread from cooking, and she always wore a bandana. I had never seen her hair because she always had that bandana on. Ta'ah also wore a long flowery dress and really thick socks. It didn't matter what the weather was like. If it was raining or snowing, she always wore a little thin sweater that she couldn't button up. She was always telling us stories and legends, and pointing out who our relatives were. I remember we would take frequent walks through the reserve. She'd say, "Let's go for a walk." We'd walk and talk, and I'd ask, "Who's that?" and she'd always say, "That's your relation." If it were a girl, I would look at her and ask, "Who is that?" and she'd without a doubt respond, "That's your *close* relation."

My Ta'ah visited all the time. She would cook for us, do our dishes and laundry. She really took care of me. Took care of us. I remember her hauling all of our laundry down the street to her place. When my Ta'ah used to comb my hair, she would spit on her hands and rub it on my head to comb the hair wet. That's just the way it was. I'd never allow anybody to do that except Ta'ah. I used to sit beside her when we ate because she would cut up my food and feed me. She also gave me the most hugs. When I was sick, if I had the flu or didn't feel well, I always went to her house. She would put me right to bed, or any one of us kids. We'd stay at her house until we got better.

My Ta'ah taught my two sisters how to weave cedar hats and cedar capes, and how to make rugs out of cloth. She was always busy doing something or cooking. Whenever it was the season to fish for salmon, we would make a big fire and Ta'ah would cook the salmon. She would cut it in a special way and tie the salmon onto pieces of wood, then hang it over the fire to barbecue it.

It was my Papa who taught me how to smoke salmon. I remember asking my Papa to read to me once. I brought him over a comic, probably Superman or Batman, and he didn't know how to read. He'd just explain to me what they were doing, as best he could. I knew that he didn't know how to read, and he would say, "Oh, this guy's doing this, and this guy's doing that," and then I'd say, "Thank you, Papa." Ta'ah was the matriarch; she made the decisions.

My grandmother, on my mom's side, lived about two doors down from an Indian Shaker Church, and she used to bring us to that. The Indian Shaker Churches were created because Indigenous beliefs were banned, so they combined those beliefs with Christianity. But my Ta'ah used to bring us to the Longhouse, which is still in the same place – on the Capilano Reserve, right by Lions Gate Bridge. Back then, when we'd visit the Longhouse, she'd pack a bunch of blankets and pillows and make a bed for us behind her because we'd go there for two to three days. We really loved it because a lot of people would come to the Longhouse. About four or five hundred folks, with about three or four hundred drums, and they would all be drumming. I remember the Longhouse just vibrating and the vibrations going right through me. It was the same thing with the Shaker Churches.

In them days, the Longhouse was quite old. I remember sitting in it, looking around at all the wall expansions. It had a lot of cedar shakes for the walls, and benches. The Longhouse was probably 120 feet long, and maybe 100 feet wide, and it could seat the crowds. The benches were stacked five high, and they went all the way around the building. There was a door in the front, and a side door leading into the kitchen. When people came to visit, the Squamish People always made sure the visitors would eat first and that we were the last to eat. There was always something to eat, and the adults made sure us kids and the Elders ate. Indigenous Peoples from down in the United States, like the Lummi, would come to the Longhouse. Even nations on Vancouver Island or from Chilliwack would come visit. People from nations all over would join.

If I am not mistaken, there have been three different Long-houses in my lifetime. Two burned down. In one instance, some bikers were seen leaving, so everyone believes they destroyed it. The other instance was accidental. I believe someone was cooking in the Longhouse and, since it was made with old dry wood, it went up like a matchbox. Once the fire started, the firemen were there to make sure it didn't spread.

Ta'ah was married twice. Her first husband was my dad's father. He passed away as a Medicine Man. He picked everything from herbs to plants and mixed them up to become medicines. She gained her knowledge about medicines from him. I remember that every so often she'd say, "I want to go for a walk now. I need medicine." All of us kids would get up and go along with her.

In them days, there were a lot of bushes and trails on the North Shore. We could walk all the way to the Lions Gate Bridge just through the trails. We'd walk along the trails and she'd say, "Oh, I want some of those," but she wouldn't pick the medicines herself – we'd go pick them. This was her way of passing knowledge on to us. We'd give them to her, and she'd say, "Taste it." Some of it tasted good and other things were kind of icky. She'd say, "Don't pick it all. We might need some later, or somebody else is going to need some." We'd bring the medicines to her, and she'd smell them. Then she'd explain to us, "This is for if your head hurts, you know, like if you've got a headache," then she'd put it in a basket, and we'd go pick some more. She'd say, "This is for if your tummy hurts," or "This is for if you've got a cut or a sore." She'd show us how to use the medicines. When she said, "Okay, I have enough now," we would make our way home.

Once we were home, Ta'ah would dump everything on the table, and tell my brother or sister to fill up a pot of water, half-full or full. Ta'ah would grab her plants, sort them out, and throw some into the pot. She then instructed my brother or sister to put it on the stove and let it boil. She was making medicine, and she was teaching us. She was teaching us all the time, sharing knowledge. "This is for when you can't sleep. Take this and it'll put you to sleep," Ta'ah would say.

The only one I remember is the mint because you could smell and taste it. Even stinging nettles were good. We called one plant skunk cabbage because it smelled like skunk. There was a big plant she used that I can't really remember the name of. I hardly ever see that plant anymore. I don't even see the same plants on the reserve these days. There are too many houses, too much cement, and too much pollution.

Back then, when the tide came in, it came all the way up to our reserve. When the tide went out, it went way out and left muddy sand with puddles about two to three inches deep. The tide went so far out it seemed like you could almost go to Vancouver – just jump in and swim across.

At times when the tide was out, my Ta'ah would make an announcement, and everyone would show up at the beach with big sticks or poles. The men would take off their shoes and roll up their pants, then we'd all line up and walk in one direction. Some of the guys would stick their poles in the big puddles, wiggle them, flip them, and a fish would go flying up. Then all of us little kids would run over, grab it, and chase it around while it was flopping. Some of the other Elders would stick their poles in the puddles, wiggle the pole around, and pull out a nice big crab. In no time, the aunties would shout to us, "Okay, we've got enough now." That meant we had enough fish or crab to feed everybody, so we'd go back up to shore and sit by the fire.

Around the fire, people would brush their feet off, then they'd put on their socks and shoes again. At this time, one of the Ta'ahs or aunties would pull out a big metal pot with a spout and handle, fill it halfway with water, and push it against the fire to boil. Then they would tell the Firekeepers – usually uncles, older men, or my brothers – to dig a hole about three or four inches deep in the sand. The Firekeepers put the crabs, clams, and fish in the hole and covered them with leaves, or sand and ash. Then they pulled the fire over top of it all, to cook the seafood. Eventually, everybody would be sitting, and the ladies would always miraculously pull out tea bags, sugar, and their cups. They put the tea bags in the hot water, then someone would go around pouring the tea.

While our catch was cooking, we would go to the cedar tree and cut bark, maybe four inches wide and about a foot long. We'd use the cedar bark as plates. The Ta'ahs would say, "Okay, it's ready," and the guys would go dig out the catch. We'd pile the food on our cedar bark. We didn't use forks or spoons to eat, either. We only needed a spoon to stir the tea. We always made sure there was something left over that we would offer to the Grandmothers and Grandfathers, and to Mother Earth. There would be two plates of food. One would be placed in the fire for our Ancestors, and one would be placed in the creek to flow away with the water, or in a tree for Mother Earth. Once we had nice full tummies, we'd all go home. There were always quite a few people at these gatherings. Sometimes it would be four or six of us, and other times about eighteen or twenty. It was a family thing.

In them days, our reserve was lush with plants and trees. There were a lot of trees – and fruit, such as salmonberries, salmonberry shoots, and blackberries, of course. In the backyard of the house where I lived with Mom and Dad, we had plum, pear, cherry, and apple trees. All of them were my favourite berries and fruit. From our windows, you could see the water. Back then, the ocean was different. It looked a lot cleaner. It looked blue or green, with white rocks and sand. We would also get about three or four feet of snow every year. I don't know, but everything seemed much cleaner. Probably because there weren't as many vehicles.

A lot of the houses were very old. They were all constructed on stilts and logs. They were built right by the water, and we used outhouses. They were built to be truly sturdy. I remember we had to walk about half a block down to get water from a little creek that no longer exists. Someone, I guess the band, hooked up a tap in the creek and we got our water there. We'd fill up a couple of buckets, or however much we needed, and bring it back home for Mom to use for cooking and cleaning. In them days, there were a lot of creeks on the reserve. We even had a creek going right beside our house.

Back then, we ate a lot of fish, chicken, and game, like deer and mountain goat. We ate quite a bit of stew, rice, potatoes and, of course, frybread or baked bread. My favourites, though, were smoked salmon, trout, and frybread. Plus, we consumed a lot of tea and homemade jams from Ta'ah's medicine trades. My Ta'ah had a whole cupboard that was filled with medicines. They had no labels on them. Visitors would go over to her house to talk. Sometimes their husbands or children were sick, and my Ta'ah would get up, open the cupboard, grab some medicine, and tell them what to do with it. The visitors would dig in their bags and give her jam or some bread, fried bread, or smoked salmon. That's how they paid. When she was teaching us, she'd say, "I'm showing you what your grandfather taught me. He told me to teach this to you kids. If you go to someone's house and they give you tea and bread, you sit down and drink the tea or eat the bread. Maybe that's all they got. And don't ever ask for anything. Don't ask for money. Just take what they give you. Sometimes they'll give you fish, maybe even half a fish, but they're sharing, they're paying. That's how some people give thanks." That's what Ta'ah taught us.

2

In Them Days

ASIDE FROM MY Ta'ah's lessons, my favourite memories from
childhood are probably the meals and hanging around with
friends. Going down to the beach, getting food, spending
summers going anywhere and everywhere. A bunch of the
kids from First Street would walk down to catch the old
ferry to Vancouver, and then we'd go to the movies. There
were four movie theatres that we'd go to. We'd watch whatever there was, since it was only about ten cents to get
admitted. We'd each bring fifty cents, which was enough for
popcorn and pop. The movies were always loaded with kids
because they showed matinees. I remember we watched Roy
Rogers and everybody's favourite, Superman. The movies
typically had cowboys-versus-Indians plots, and because of
this, I always felt that the Indians were bad. In those movies,
the Indians were killing people in massacres. I didn't like it.
I felt guilty because I was an Indian. It wasn't the same in
Roy Rogers and Gene Autry movies. They never really killed
anybody, like in the other kind of movies. Instead, they
always shot the gun out of their enemy's hand rather than
kill them. So those were good movies.

During the summertime, us kids would stay outside until
the sun went down, or until we could hear our parents calling

us in. We would go catch salmon or trout, or pick clams and crabs, then cook them. I would go around with Rick, who was my age, and my older brother Andy. I called Rick my brother because he lived right next door to us. When we weren't at his house, he was always at our house. There was also Patty – he was my age – a guy named Harold – we called him Cookie – who was about the same age as my brother Andy, a guy called Big Brian, and Louie Miranda. That's the thing; we travelled around a lot together, in a little gang of all the guys around our age. We went swimming and fishing, and walked downtown. We frequented the ocean because when the tide went out, there was a big area we could use to swim. We'd walk along the train tracks and go down to Mosquito Creek to swim and fish, but most of the time we stayed below the church and swam there because we loved the sand. We used a hook and string to fish. We used what we called seaworms as bait, tied a rock around the string to use as a sinker, then dropped the line in. We caught sockeye salmon, spring salmon, and some dogfish in Mosquito Creek. Maybe somebody had a nickel or dime and we'd get a pop, go sit in a bush or on a chair, and share it. Also, there was a mill right beside the reserve and we knew the guys who worked there. We'd go talk to them sometimes. They knew us by name, and we knew them by name. As kids, we always found things to do or play with, you know?

I remember we had this dog, this rez dog. His name was Prince. I think he was the last dog that the people used to make wool from. People on the rez had dogs that they used to cut the fur of to make wool. Prince used to follow us kids around. He was part of our gang. As soon as we got up in the morning, he'd be sitting outside waiting for us. We'd sit outside, eating whatever we had, and give him toast or whatever.

Our family had a dog too. She was a water spaniel and her name was Sugar. She was born around the same time as me. She passed away when she was about fifteen. She was a part of the family. One time, she had puppies and Mom put them outside on the back porch. We were all in bed one particular night when we heard Sugar growling and fighting. Mom bolted outside to see what was going on. There were about four rats trying to get the newborn pups, and Sugar was fending them off. So Mom, Dad, and Ross started clubbing away the rats. My dad had said he wanted to get rid of the puppies, but he still went out there with a stick to fend off the rats. Thankfully, they never got any puppies, and Mom moved the puppies inside. We always had a cat or a dog to keep the rats out of the house.

Another time when I was a kid, our cat had kittens on my brother Andy's pillow – right by his head. Me and my brother used to sleep together, and I woke up one morning and the cat – we called her Tipsy – had given birth to four tiny kittens. There was blood and afterbirth everywhere, including on my brother's head, and all the kittens were mewing. I yelled for my mom and she got a box and a blanket and put them in there. Tipsy was a tabby cat and this was one of her first litters. She kept having kittens, and her later litters were more like eight or nine kittens. Eventually, we just had a box under the stove; it was the kitten box.

Once in a while we helped Mom with chores. It was mostly our mess, I guess. We'd tidy up our toys and our clothes, and she'd do the laundry. Sometimes my sister and I would go out to help Mom hang clothes on the clothesline. We'd stand beside her and hand her the clothespins. Dad, on the other hand, if he was ever building something, we could only pretend we were helping.

I remember that every Friday, Dad got paid, so that was a big thing. My mom and all my aunties would meet at our house, and one auntie would stay home with all of us kids. Usually one or two aunties would stay home to watch about ten of us kids. There was Auntie Micky, Auntie Dorothy, Auntie Mabel, and Auntie Bunny. My mom and aunties would get ready, put their makeup on. They'd go meet my dad and their husbands. Their husbands were longshoremen, too, and had the same payday. Mom would come home with these little cardboard wax boxes, and they were always filled with Chinese food. Everyone was always so happy because we'd all be sitting around eating Chinese food. After supper, Mom would put a blanket on the floor and dump all the toys she bought us. I think the ladies would go to second-hand stores. They'd leave at about seven in the morning and be gone all day. When they got home, they would have a whole bunch of shopping bags. Mom would buy whatever anybody needed. They weren't new toys, but we would pick whatever we wanted. I remember I had an old brown teddy bear with one eye. I'm sure Mom got it from a second-hand store because it was pretty beat-up when I got it. I didn't care, though. It was my buddy, and I slept with it.

I seemed to get sick a lot as a kid. Whenever pneumonia was going around, I got it. When the flu was going around, I got flu. I also had an ear problem, a mastoid, that bothered me until it was operated on. I can recall my mom getting me dressed early one morning when I was about four and taking me on the bus to St. Paul's Hospital in Vancouver. At the time, I didn't have a clue where we were going. Before we got to the hospital, she brought me into a grocery store and bought me a pop. After that, she walked me to the hospital and left me there. The hospital had a detergent smell to it. The nurses led me up to my room, and of course I was terrified. I cried a lot, and the doctors took quite a bit of blood. A couple days later, on the day of the operation, I remember trying to fight them off when they were putting me to sleep. The hospital staff had to hold me down, and I was even trying to hold my breath. They finally put me to sleep once they got the mask on and completed the operation on my ear. I don't know how long it was, but I seemed to stay in the hospital for a long time. Thankfully, the nurses were pleasant and nice. They were there to take care of me. I had no fear of them, even though they were nuns. Back then, I just knew that they were Christian or something.

I was quite happy back then, you know? Being young, I didn't know whether it was Monday, Tuesday, Wednesday, or Thursday. I would just go to bed, wake up when the sun was shining, and carry on. I didn't know any days, but I remember enjoying things because I'd get up with my siblings, sometimes even my dad. Mom would be cooking breakfast, mostly eggs, bacon, and toast, or just eggs and toast with a bottle of milk. In addition, at that time, there were only two TVs on the reserve that I knew of. One of them was at my Ta'ah's house and we used to go over there to watch. There would be a whole bunch of us, the whole family. There were about two channels. We watched shows like *Howdy Doody*.

In them days, I didn't really have a sense of the world outside of the reserve and North Vancouver because I was mostly hanging around with a crowd from the reserve. We stuck with each other, and at the time there were probably about two hundred people living on the rez. We didn't really communicate with people off the reserve, unless we gave them money or we bought something. When I think about it, we didn't really have many interactions with white people. I think I must have been pretty well protected because I didn't know about the outside world. It didn't really concern me. It wasn't until I went to residential school that I was taught that we were different. Residential school taught me that the priests, the RCMP, and the nuns were number one. They were the rule. The boss.

But it wasn't like that prior to residential school. Before residential school, I never felt unsafe around white people. They had grocery stores, corner stores. We just went to the store, and if they were there, they were there. They drove the taxis and ran the ferries. They seemed to all be in service work. We never went out of our way to connect with white people, unless they talked to us. I remember my dad took us to the movies on Saturdays, and he would talk to the white guys. When we were on the ferry, the guys would say, "Hey, hi," and he'd go over to talk to them.

But there was one time when I learned something about the difference between white people and us. When I was about four or five years old, I was playing outside, and I walked away from our yard toward a shingle mill where some other boys were playing. They climbed the boxcars – the ones that carried shingles – and then they started jumping from the boxcars to the mill, which was about three feet away. At first, I was too scared to jump, but the other boys urged me on, so I took a little run and jumped. I was surprised how easy it was, so I jumped back onto the boxcar and back to the mill and I kept going back and forth. It seemed easy, so I got careless, and then I jumped back to the boxcar from the mill without taking a run and I didn't make it. I hit the ground hard. I lay there dazed. When I got up, my chin was bleeding and my arm just hung there. I started walking toward home. I must have been in shock. As I walked, I seen my mom and dad and my whole family running toward me. My mom got to me first and then my dad scooped me up. I thought I'd get spanked, so I tried to blame my brother, who wasn't even there when I fell. They carried me home and they must have called a taxi to rush me to Lions Gate Hospital.

In them days, Lions Gate couldn't or wouldn't help Natives. I lay there on a bed, bleeding and crying, with my arm broken. Three doctors stood by the door and did nothing but watch me. My dad got angry and yelled, "What kind of doctors are you?" But they just stood there. Finally, a nurse came rushing forward. She said she didn't care about the rules, and she poked me with a painkiller. One of the doctors yelled at her, but she glared back and left the room. My pain started to go away and then an ambulance took me to Vancouver to St. Paul's Hospital – the Indian hospital. I remember the siren and that the ambulance seemed to go very fast. My mom kept telling me to lie down. The next thing I remember was waking up with my arm in a cast and my mom and dad standing by my bed and looking worried. Then a nurse came and gave me another needle and I fell back to sleep. Even today, my right arm is still bent at the elbow. The surgeons did the best they could, but it's never been the same.

Even though our parents worried about us, they weren't really affectionate while we were growing up. I'm a second-generation residential school Survivor, so there wasn't much physical or verbal affection in our house. No one ever said "I love you" and I don't think me and my siblings bonded that much, even though we loved each other. We still do. When I was a kid, my mom didn't pick me up much, but I do have some memories of her packing me around when I was very young. We never got any hugs from Dad either – except sometimes when he drank, he would hug us. My parents never talked about their lives, and when I went off to residential school, even though they'd gone, we never talked about it. When I was at the school, we were occasionally allowed to come home for the weekends, and once, when my dad brought us back to the school on Sunday evening, he asked, "How do they treat you there?" I said it was okay and that was it. I was afraid to tell him about the abuse because if ever we complained about it, and the nuns found out, we'd get slapped or get the strap. If my dad didn't believe what I said, he didn't say anything about it.

As a family, we did take a couple of trips that I can recall. We went to Upper Squamish, because Dad had family up there. We also went deer hunting with our dad in Upper Squamish. He always shot the deer and we didn't actually do anything. Us kids always stayed behind him. We'd follow his lead, watch his moves, and learn how to be quick and quiet. Another time, we attended canoe races down in the United States. The races took place in Lummi, Washington, or a little bit farther south. We got a motel for the night. All the canoe racers from across the Lower Mainland competed there in six-man races. It was a big occasion. Of course, there was plenty of salmon, crabs, and clams to go around.

Before all the kids in my age group went to residential school, there wasn't a lot of alcohol use on the rez, but the adults did occasionally party. I remember my uncles and aunties would come over and the adults would drink or go out. It was once we went away to the school that there was a surge in alcohol use on the reserve among my parents' generation. I believe it was because they no longer had children to take care of.

Before residential school, I didn't know much about Christianity. I think we went to church once in a while. We usually went on occasions like Easter and Christmas. We'd go with my parents or my grandmother. Christmas was a big time because the church had midnight Mass, and we'd go as a family. I do remember that the priest had a sort of bank for the kids to save money in. If we had a quarter, we'd give him the quarter, and he'd put a little stamp in a book we had to log our savings. I also remember going to the church grave-yard. That was when we sort of experienced Christianity. The cemetery had a section right at the end of the graveyard reserved for the deceased that weren't baptized. They had to be buried by themselves because they weren't Christian. I knew that my siblings and I were baptized.

Before I went to the school, I didn't know much about it. I have memories of kids disappearing, like Patty, Cookie, and Louie. I remember my brother telling me that they were gone to the school. I'd ask my mom about what happened to my friends, and she wouldn't say they went to residential school. She'd just say, "They're gone to school." I knew that meant they went to live there. It was as if people were saying that the kids went to a bad place without saying those exact words. Even my dad – once in a while he would say, "I went to residential school," but he never elaborated on what that meant. Maybe my parents never talked about it because they had a bad experience or maybe they didn't want to scare us. It wasn't until my siblings and I went that we would see everyone who disappeared.

3

Our Lives
Signed Away

I **REMEMBER MY** first day of residential school vividly. I remember that I was playing at home on the floor of the living room with my brother Andy, when there was a knock on the door.

It was a strange thing because on the reserve no one ever knocked. I remember my parents opening the door and a man coming inside and talking to them. Whatever they were talking about seemed to make my mom really upset and my dad really cross. I looked the strange man up and down. He was an older white guy. He had gray hair combed right back. He wore glasses, a kind of heavy suit jacket, and brown pants. I came to know that his name was Mr. Taylor and he was an Indian agent.

After talking to my parents at the front door for a few minutes, Mr. Taylor made his way into the house. I didn't understand what they had been talking about, but I remember having the sense that it was about us kids. Shortly thereafter – days or weeks – my mom got all of us kids together and said, "Put your coats and your shoes on. You're going with your dad." I don't know why my older siblings hadn't gone to school before me, but we did what we were told; we all got dressed up and made our way out the front door. I didn't know where we were going. I remember walking away from our house and looking back at my mom standing on the porch. She looked so sad, like she was going to cry. We kept on walking.

My best guess was that we were walking to my Ta'ah and Papa's house. My brother Andy and I walked a little behind, goofing around and play-fighting, the way boys do. My dad, who walked holding my sisters' hands, seemed off, but I paid no mind. By this time, my oldest brother, Ross, was around fifteen and working with my dad as a longshoreman, so he wasn't with us. We walked the half a block to my Ta'ah's house, but when we got there, we walked past it. We walked another block, to the foot of the hill. I looked up at Andy, who was looking back at me. We both knew what was on top of that hill, casting a shadow over the reserve. We knew that all the kids who walked up that hill disappeared. Andy and I joined our dad and sisters in silence, and we solemnly walked the final two blocks up the hill to our new residence, four blocks from our house: St. Paul's Indian Residential School.

When we got to the school, we walked up a set of old, worn-out stairs. The school was really old and dingy. It was a greyish-white colour, and all the paint was cracked and peeling. When we got to the top of the stairs, there was a door. My dad knocked. A nun named Mother Michaela, who was the school's principal, opened the door and told us kids to sit down. She was a tall, thin-faced woman, maybe in her fifties, with really sharp features. She wore glasses, and you could tell by the way she spoke that she was in charge, that if you disobeyed her, there would be consequences. I never saw her smile.

My dad walked into her office, and I could see him signing papers. I didn't know it then, but he was signing our lives away. When he was finished, he walked out of the office, looked down at us. "You kids listen, and you be good."

He turned toward Mother Michaela. "Take good care of my kids."

And then he left. He never said goodbye. He never hugged us. He just turned around and walked out. I'm sure he and my mom weren't happy when we went off. Maybe they hoped it would be different for us. I remember being confused and scared. I remember that feeling of being abandoned. It was a lot for a seven-year-old. Little did I know that it was only the beginning of the trauma that would suffocate my innocence and change my life forever. It would be a long time before I would ever have the opportunity to process what was happening to my siblings and me.

Before we knew it, two nuns came in, one for my sisters and one for me and my brother. They led us off in separate ways. These nuns looked scary, alien. They wore long black tunics with a hood-like headdress. Each of them had a big rosary and silver cross hanging from their hip, and on their other hip they had a strap. The strap was a piece of leather or rubber, maybe a foot long and about a quarter inch thick by about two inches wide; it was used specifically to beat the kids. All the nuns always carried their straps hanging from their hip. We followed the nun with her strap through a huge dining hall. There were three or four big old tables with benches on each side, and a divider in the middle of the room, with a similar layout on the other side. I saw into a kitchen that had a big, long wood-burning stove. We kept following her up a set of stairs. I could see the paint peeling and feel the wetness of the old wood in my nose. The stairs led into a dark hallway. There wasn't even a light in the hallway. She looked at us, told Andy to wait where he was, and instructed me to follow her. She led me into a big dormitory. I took in the room and saw all the single-sized cots lined up in a row. She motioned to a bed and told me that every time I was brought to this room, I was to go to this bed. I sat down on the bed. The nun left the room and, unbeknownst to me, did the same routine with my brother in a different dormitory. I was glued to the bed. My eyes searched the dimly lit room. A single light bulb illuminated the whole room. There was a small bathroom in the corner of the room, which looked to have four or five sinks and a metal wall that functioned as a mirror. At the end of the row of beds, there was one small window. At something like one foot by two feet, and covered by a drawn curtain, it didn't add much brightness to the room. I felt paralyzed.

When the nun came back, she told me to take my clothes off. Once I was naked, she grabbed my clothes and told me to follow her again. I followed her into a curtained-off area they called the medicine room. When I walked into the room, my brother was sitting in a chair wrapped in a bedsheet. The man standing above him, with shears in his hands, had just shaved his head. The man took off and shook out the sheet that had covered Andy and motioned for me to take my brother's place. Andy, who stood about four feet away from me, stared at me blankly. He kept staring until the nun asked him to cover his eyes with one hand and his mouth with the other. When he had done as she had asked, she took some sort of pump and started spraying him down with a white powder. She sprayed him everywhere: front and back, under his feet, and in between his legs. They wanted us to be white so badly. When he was caked in the stuff, another nun came and grabbed him, and, without being prompted, I knew what I was to do. And so I stood in Andy's footprints and she started spraying me. I thought to myself that it must be some kind of strong detergent because of the smell. It made me feel dizzy and nauseous. After she was done, she gave me instructions not to touch it or clean it off, assuring me that it would naturally come off. I found out some time later that it was pesticide.

Covered in pesticide, I followed the nun back to the dormitory, where there sat a stack of clothes on my bed. She told me to get dressed. While doing so, I noticed that all the clothes had the number *3* embroidered on them. All the children at the school got numbers: the boys got odd numbers and the girls got even numbers. I was number 3. A lot of the time, the nuns wouldn't even use your name. They would just say, "Hey, number 3, come over here."

After I was dressed, I followed the nun once again, this time to a classroom downstairs. The classroom, which was for grades 1, 2, and 3, was huge. All of the desks were big and heavy, and made of cast iron. The walls were lined with all of the school's new kids, while the centre of the room was occupied by playing children. The playing children were inside because it was pouring rain. I saw my brother and quickly made my way over to sit beside him. We didn't say anything. Rather, we scanned the room, making note of all the children. Some of them were our friends and cousins who had disappeared from the reserve. Some even came over and said hi to us. We sat there until one of the nuns rang a bell. All the kids stopped playing immediately and formed a line. Not knowing what to do, all of us new kids just sat there. The nun who had taken my clothes and sprayed me down informed us that we were to line up based on our assigned numbers, sharing that if you had a little brother, you were to help him find his place in the line.

Single file, we made our way into the dining hall that I had walked through earlier. I thought we were supposed to sit, but a boy put his hand out in front of me, telling me to stay in the line. Beyond the divider that separated the room into two, I could see the girls coming into the room. The divider was used to segregate the girls and boys. I remember looking for my little sister – Honey Bee – in the crowd. I spotted her and started to wave, but she wouldn't look at me. She just looked straight ahead. A nun ran over to me.

"Don't look around! Either you look straight ahead or you look down," she said in a raised voice. After all of the girls had entered the room, I bowed my head and looked down as all of us children knelt and prayed to their god.

I sat at the table looking at my rudimentary dishware. One small plate – it couldn't have been much bigger than my outstretched seven-year-old hand – with high edges, a spoon, and a metal cup. I stared at it. All of the older girls helped the nuns prepare the meals. One of them, pushing a cart with a big round pot on it, served us our supper. She took my plate and put my food on it. Getting it back, I saw that there were two pieces of stew meat, two carrots, and some potato and celery all in hot, greasy water. The next older girl gave each of us a piece of bread with margarine, and another helper girl filled up our cups with powdered milk. When we were done, we prayed to their god again, thanking him for the meal. That was the meal I ate, and the routine I followed, for lunch and supper every day for the eight years I spent at St. Paul's.

After our meal was finished, and because the rain hadn't let up, all of us students made our way back into the big classroom again. A short time later, we were told to go to our dormitories, put our pyjamas on, and get ready for bed. It was 6:30 on an early September evening. It was still light out when we had to say the final prayer of the day. Before leaving the room, the nun gave us strict instructions not to talk or move, and to go right to sleep. She turned out the light and we all got into our beds. She left the room but opened a curtain covering an interior window to let us all know that she was watching us from her adjacent bedroom. When the nun would open her curtain, we all knew to pretend we were sleeping. Of course, as soon as she closed the curtain, we all popped up and started talking. I already knew a lot of the kids. Most of them were from my reserve. The kids we didn't know would tell us who they were and where they were from. The building was so old and creaky that every time a nun made her way to check on us, we'd be back in our sleeping positions and quiet by the time she was scanning the dormitory. They did this a couple times a night, just to make sure we knew that they, like their god, were always watching us.

We were woken every morning by the ring of a bell at six thirty. Once we were dressed in our numbered outfits, we would file our way into the chapel for morning prayer. The boys and girls sat segregated in the right and left rows of pews. All of the prayers we sang were out of a book called the hymnal. The whole book was written in Latin. In all my time at the school, not once did a nun ever even attempt to explain what the words we were reciting meant. My native language was forbidden – I would forget any knowledge I had of it – but by the time I left St. Paul's eight years later, after I had been forced to become an altar boy, I could recite all of Mass perfectly in Latin. The nuns all spoke in French. That did little to hide the fact that they were talking about us.

After chapel, all of the kids would do the chores they were assigned. Once everyone had completed their chores, the bell would ring yet again, signalling to us to make our way to the dining hall for breakfast. Like at supper, we all filled the two separate sides of the room. I didn't try to wave at Honey Bee anymore. I knew to either look down or look straight ahead. We also were not allowed to speak during mealtimes. To be frank, I never had any compliments to give to the chef anyway. For breakfast, an older girl pushing the cart would plop a scoop of mush on our plate – it was either oatmeal or cream of wheat or something along those lines – with one piece of bread and one cup of powdered milk. If ever there was a special visitor at the school, we would get cornflakes or puffed wheat. We were all growing children, and the meals did little to satisfy our hunger. One time, a little boy – he must have been four or five years old – asked one of the nuns if he could have some more food. She didn't just say no, she made a scene of it. In front of everyone, she really scolded the poor kid. "Go and sit down, fat-boy," she said to the hungry boy. The cruellest part was that you could see the food carts that went into where the nuns and priests, who did Mass at the church we went to, ate. They had pancakes, eggs, bacon, toast, milk, and sugar – you name it. Some of the boys would even wait until all the nuns and priests left the dining room so that they could go in there and eat their scraps out of the garbage. These kids were so jubilant to get a piece of scrap bacon or toast. I only ever tried to do it once. My brother Andy saw me and stopped me.

"I don't want to see you eating anybody's garbage," he whispered to me.

And so I never did, even though I was always hungry. To say the food left something to be desired is putting it lightly. Most of the time, we were listening to the nuns, but some of the time, we were listening to our empty stomachs. You learned quickly that this was the way it was. We were not to ask the nuns for anything. We were to listen, all the while trying to retain some sense of dignity. This was how I spent most every day between the ages of seven and fourteen, confined within the walls of St. Paul's. Of course, some days and experiences I had while at the school deviated from the repetitively mundane cruelty that all us kids suffered. Some were bad, some were good, but all of them should never have had to happen to anyone, let alone children.

4

The Strap

ST. PAUL'S GROUNDS were fenced, and all along the fence, just like by my house, were fruit trees of different varieties. There were apple trees, pear trees, cherry trees, and plum trees, all bursting with fruit. You could see ripe pieces of fruit littering the ground along the fence, but out of fear of the nuns' wrath, no one dared venture to grab them. That is, until one day, when my Uncle Willard, my mom's brother, who was also a student at St. Paul's, came up and grabbed me and another boy and snuck us behind one of the school's walls during playtime in the schoolyard. He told us the plan.

"Okay, Sam, you're going to go to that corner, and you, you go to that corner. If you see a nun, don't holler, but let us know that she's coming as soon as you see her."

The boy and I took our posts. About three or four older boys and Willard walked down to the fence, flipped their shirts to make baskets, and filled up their makeshift baskets with apples and pears. After their harvest, we all helped gather some younger kids and, being careful not to get caught, made our way to the basement to enjoy the fruit. My uncle gave me a whole apple and pear. If there wasn't enough to go around, the older boys would break their fruit in half; everybody got some. You ate all of it, too – the core, seeds, and stem – so that nobody got caught. That was what the older boys did. They always tried to take care of us. They always did their best, but sometimes that wasn't enough.

My sister Margaret would sometimes sneak me a treat. She worked in the kitchen – they cooked for us, and they cooked for the nuns and priests, and sometimes, if the nuns and priests didn't eat something, she would take it for us. It was only toast or something like that, but it was something we never got.

My first day in lessons, I was sitting at one of those cast-iron desks. I was in the third of four rows from the front. Behind me, in the fourth row, was a kid my age and his older brother. I could hear them talking but couldn't understand what they were saying. They were Musqueam and they were speaking in their language. It seemed like the older brother was giving his little brother some instructions. Whatever they were talking about, they were too deep in conversation to notice that a nun was standing right behind them. Without warning she wound up her yardstick and started hitting them on their heads. They both started wailing, crying, and screaming. She beat them so hard with that yardstick that it flew out of her hands, at which point she leaned over and started closed-fist punching the floored kids. When she got tired, she grabbed them and dragged them to the front of the classroom and made them kneel, facing us.

"These boys were speaking their language. You are never to do that again! If you speak that language, you're talking to the devil! You're calling the devil into your life and you're going to go to Hell forever!"

For the rest of the class, the brothers had to stay kneeling where they were. We were all really quiet and really scared. We were always scared in class. The nuns taught us regular subjects like English, math, science, and social studies, but if we didn't learn fast enough or if we got something wrong, we'd get slapped or we'd be made to kneel down. I don't know if the quality of education was any worse than a regular school. We spent plenty of time learning, but the threat of punishment was always there.

Once, in one of those earlier years, I heard Honey Bee crying when we were in class. I looked over and there was a nun pulling her by the ear and slapping her on the wrist. She was slapping my sister's wrist because she was left-handed and was supposed to be writing with her right hand. I was vibrating mad, staring over at my sister getting punished. I wanted so badly to go over there, punch that nun, and tell her to leave my sister alone, but before I knew it, Rick and my brother Andy ran over. They stood on either side of the nun, throwing as many punches as they could get in before they were surrounded and beaten down by the other nuns. They did the exact same thing in my defence whenever the nuns decided I was going to get a whupping. Each time, they succeeded in taking the beating off us young ones, even if it was just for a second. And each time, they got the strap for it.

We all got the strap – it was the one thing in that place that didn't discriminate. The first time I got the strap, I was playing in the yard and a nun called out, "Number 3!" When I looked up, she said, "Come here." When I got to her, she led me up a set of stairs into the grades 1, 2, and 3 classroom.

"Kneel down," she told me. I did as she instructed, but when she reached for the strap on her hip, she realized she had forgotten it in her room.

"Stay where you are," she said, as she made her way to her room to grab it. Just after she left, my Uncle Willard – who had been watching from around a corner – snuck into the room. He knew what was happening.

"Put your hands out," he said. I did as he directed. He spat in my hands.

"Rub them together," he said. I was sure he was tricking me. He was a few years older than I was and he was always teasing me. Certain that this was another one of his jokes, I made to wipe my hands off on my shirt. He stopped me.

"You're going to get the strap. Rub them together," he told me.

"When you put your hands out, tilt them like this," he said, positioning his hands so that his fingernails were closer to the floor.

"Cause your hands are wet, when the nun hits you, it's not going to hurt," Willard explained. The creaky old building was telling us that the nun was getting closer. Willard gave me his final instruction: "When she's hitting you, stare her in the face." With that, he ran out the door, but not before teasingly telling me not to cry or he'd beat me up.

The nun walked in the room with the strap in her hand. "Put your hands out," she ordered.

Having been put somewhat at ease by my uncle, I just stared back at her with a smirk on my face. This isn't going to hurt, I thought to myself. Turned out that my uncle lied to me. It hurt very badly, but I didn't let it show. I just stared her in the face and made sure not to cry. I wasn't going to give her the satisfaction. This only seemed to make her madder and the strapping more intense. What's worse is that she never told me what I was getting the strap for. If I had known what I had done, I could have at least tried not to do it again. As the years went on, any time I would get the strap, I would pull my hands out as the nuns were swinging downwards and they would whack themselves in the leg. When I did that, I got hit a few extra times, but they were definitely gentler smacks because the nun knew that you might pull your hands out. I was learning how to take care of myself, and that meant I was learning to look out for the younger kids too.

Having my Uncle Willard at school meant he always knew when it was my birthday. It's on June 17, and his is on the 16th. He gave me what he called the royal bumps. That meant he grabbed both my feet and dragged me down the stairs, and he'd laugh. I'd try not to cry, and he'd rub my head and laugh.

Another memory I have of being with my family at school is the time I was on a swing with my other uncle – Uncle Jack, Willard's younger brother. He was my age. We were on the swing together and, of course, he had to go high. We both pumped our legs to make the swing go higher and higher. Then the chain broke. I still remember the look of fear on Jack's face as we flew through the air. I bet I had the same look. Then the hard ground met us. I got lucky, though, because my uncle Jack was chubby and I landed on top of him. Still, we both had the wind knocked out of us and had to stagger around trying to catch our breath. Next thing I know, I heard Uncle Willard laughing at us – I guess you can call that Indian sympathy. The next day I noticed that Uncle Jack had a fat lip and a swollen chin. I laughed at him – more Indian sympathy. I told him he looked like a pelican, which he didn't like so much. Still, for the whole week, I called him pelican. We both recovered and I don't think I ever swung like that again. Another lesson learned the hard way at residential school.

The only relief we'd get from the school was on the weekends we'd be allowed to go home. On the weekends when we had to stay at school, we had to do chores. We had to scrub the walls, the windows, and the floors of the classrooms and the dormitories. In the dorms, we'd have to move all the beds aside, push them tight together, and get on our hands and knees and scrub the floor from one end to the other. Then someone else – usually the younger boys – would have to wipe the floors dry with a rag. This would take up most of

Saturday, from morning until late afternoon, and all the children had to work.

Another thing at school that could have been nice was Monday nights, which were movie nights. But there was a nun – Sister Rose – and she was unpredictable. She could be nice but had a mean streak in her. For some reason, and we never knew why, Sister Rose would gather us in the classroom on Monday nights to say the rosary, and then she wouldn't let us go to the movie. Instead, we'd have to sit at our desks until the movie was over and then we had to go straight to bed. She knew when the movie was over because she always let one boy – the same boy each time – go to the movie by himself. She never told us why she was punishing the rest of us, but she would sit in the teacher's desk watching us, hoping to catch someone talking or moving. We didn't get too many luxuries at St. Paul's, but movie night was one of them, and for whatever reason, she took that away.

5

A Girl Named Pearl,
a Boy Named Charlie

WHEN I WAS ABOUT eight or nine, I got very sick. Double pneumonia. I almost died. I remember Mother Michaela took my temperature and put me to bed in the little boys' dorm, which was where everyone went when they were sick. My older sister Margaret came to see me; she looked worried, and then the nuns started dressing me. They took me by taxi to St. Paul's Hospital. Margaret came with me and Mother Michaela to the hospital.

I remember they had to take blood and they couldn't find my vein. It was quite painful. They kept poking and poking and I was crying. Margaret was brushing my hair and telling me, "It's okay." I stayed in the hospital for about two months. My dad came to see me at the hospital and my mom came too. By this time, my parents had both started drinking and had split up. My dad was living in North Vancouver and my mom in Upper Squamish. My oldest brother, Ross, came to see me too. I finally left the hospital at Easter time.

When I was a little older, around ten or eleven years old, a girl named Pearl came to St. Paul's. I think she was no older than fourteen, maybe thirteen. She was very quiet and subdued, and alone, always alone. It didn't seem like she had any friends at the school. She looked – not troubled, but sad or something. I don't know where she was from; she just showed up one day, and then one day she disappeared. I once asked my sister if she remembered Pearl and where she was from. My sister wasn't sure, but she thought Pearl might have been from Mount Currie.

There was nothing remarkable about her. She wore the same school garb as everyone else. I can't remember how long her hair was, or what she looked like, but she'd talk to me. In them days, I was Sammy and I'd walk by her and she'd wave and say, "Hi, Sammy." Or when I was running, she'd say, "Run, Sammy, run!" I think she might have related to me a little bit because she seen me being hit around – abused – physically and verbally by the nuns. I seen her abused too – everyone was – but I think she liked me. Maybe because I was sort of alone too. I did play with the other kids, but I sat alone a lot too.

Then one day she was gone. I never seen her around again. We were informed that she ran away – I think the nuns told us that – I'm not sure. No one talked about her. She just disappeared and no one ever really knew her.

When kids ran away, they ran away for a reason. I figured she'd had enough and took off. If anyone ever did run away, it was at about five o'clock in the morning. We had fire escapes and we knew how to open them. They had little buzzers on them, and we used to put gum on the buzzers so that you could just open the doors and close them again without the buzzers going off.

Today I think there's a good chance that Pearl died at the school. There's a good possibility that she ran away too. A lot of girls, when they ran away, ended up in the Downtown Eastside. Pearl came into my mind recently when I heard something about the missing and murdered women and girls. She's basically the only one I knew who went missing, and I always wondered about her. I don't know her last name, but she wasn't Squamish, so her name isn't even on the memorial (at the site of the former St. Paul's school).

Since St. Paul's was so close to our home, we got to go home for Christmas and Easter. I remember one of the early Christmases back home wasn't so good because my dad had broken up with my mom and we had nothing. We had no toys. That year I wrapped up my toys and my brother wrapped up his toys and we gave them to each other. We tried to make Christmas happier. My older sister and Ross would do their best, but my dad was into alcohol by then, so the older siblings had to take care of us younger ones.

Back at school one day, I was playing in the yard with three or four other boys when we saw the nuns walking a new kid in. We all ran toward the little boy. He was wearing a little sailor's outfit – the kind with the white American sailor's hat, the bib on the back, and the pants flared. He was a cute little guy. He looked to be about three years old.

"Number 3, this is Charlie," said the nun. He was so fresh at the school that he didn't even have a number yet. "I want you to take care of him," the nun said. I was chosen simply because I had been the first one to make it to Charlie and the nun when they walked in. So I took little Charlie under my wing, and he became like my shadow. The other boys used to say that Charlie was my puppy because he followed me everywhere I went.

I took pride in being Charlie's protector. I helped him do everything. We'd get to shower once a week and I would help get him undressed and ready for the shower. I'd have to shampoo his hair and my hair quickly under the freezing cold water. His lip would be quivering because the shower was so cold. I would rub his hair hard and fast and try to get him to warm up. I'd try to get his mind off it. I'd tickle him, or we would do this bit where, when I was helping him get dressed, I would put his shoe on the wrong foot. He'd say, "No, not like that," and we'd have a laugh together. I took really good care of him.

Playing war was a favourite pastime of the boys at the school. We'd all run around with our crooked little sticks pretending they were army rifles. I remember the time when Charlie was in the enemy army. I made sure that I spotted him and that when our armies ran toward each other in battle, I would come face-to-face with him. When he saw me, he ran at me excitedly with his crooked little stick aimed to shoot. Charlie was so young and uncoordinated, he looked funny and awkward, but I let him take his shot. "BANG," he said, smiling from ear to ear. It made his day. After the battle, we made off to relax. There were hills all over the school grounds and, seeing that it was a nice day, Charlie and I went to lay our heads in the grass on the far side of one of them. We found a nice spot out of view of the nuns and traded our makeshift rifles for a nice juicy brown pear that I had cautiously picked off a tree. I broke it in two and gave Charlie a half. I told him to eat the whole thing and to not let the nuns know anything about the fruit. We ate the ripened fruit under the warm sun. After we finished, full of happiness, we closed our eyes and rested our heads. I woke up to the sound of the whistle that signalled to us that it was time to come inside. My eyes opened to find Charlie's head on my chest. Here he was, this little three-year-old, with his little mouth, nose, and lips. I shook him gently to wake him up.

"Charlie, we got to go in now," I told him as I brushed away any bit of pear he had stuck to his face. The little guy stretched out and rubbed his eyes the way toddlers do. After reminding him again to not tell Sister that we had eaten a pear, we walked back to the school together. I really loved taking care of Charlie and making him smile.

I bring up Charlie because he didn't make it. He's one of the ones who died in there. The last time I saw Charlie, I was lying in my bed and heard him crying. I looked over at him and I could see that he was holding his head. I got out of my bed and went over to him.

"What's wrong, Charlie?" I asked, concerned.

"My head hurts," he answered. I didn't say anything back to him. Being careful that no nun was near, I took him in my arms, and softly rubbed his head. Soon enough he stopped crying and then fell asleep. I tucked him back in and went back to my bed. I felt really worried about him, so I stayed awake for a long time, just watching him, making sure he was okay. After an hour or so, I drifted off to sleep.

When I woke up, his blankets were pushed away and his bed was empty. He was gone. I found out that he had been rushed to the hospital in the middle of the night. When Mother Michaela gathered all the boys to tell us what happened to Charlie, all she shared was that he had had a brain tumour and that he died on the operating table. Later, I heard that he had to have the top of his skull cut off. That was the reason we weren't allowed to see his body at the funeral. Another thing about his funeral was that the school didn't know where Charlie was from. He had a sister at the school, but all she knew was that they had come to St. Paul's by boat. Their mother had dropped them off and the sister had no idea where she had gone after that. Because of that, his funeral and burial were on our reserve.

It wasn't until I was about sixty that my brother Rick brought up Charlie. I'd gone to visit Rick for the last time, as he was terminally ill.

"Remember that little boy? The one we used to call your puppy," he asked.

"Yeah," I replied.

Rick told me that the day before Charlie went to hospital, he and another boy had been playing upstairs near the dormitories where they were not supposed to be. When they heard someone coming near, assuming it was a nun, they looked for a place to hide and squeezed in between a big dresser and the wall. Rick explained to me that he saw a nun come into the room with her hand wrapped around Charlie's arm, dragging him along behind her. Rick said that he couldn't really make out what she was saying to Charlie, but he saw her start to hit and then shake him. And then, Rick said, he saw her throw him down the stairs as she shook him.

He was an innocent little boy who was hurt by a grown woman who felt she was entitled to do so by God.

Charlie's funeral started with a High Mass at the big church that was on the reserve, not the one on the school grounds. After the service, I followed behind some of the bigger boys as they carried the little casket. Everybody walking, myself included, was saying prayers and singing songs in Latin. We got to the graveyard and I stood by Charlie's grave, watching as they lowered his casket. For the first time, I understood what death was, the finality of it. Charlie was gone. When the kids started to throw dirt on top of his coffin, it brought me to tears. All the children lined up, each one taking a handful of earth and throwing it on top of Charlie. When everyone was finished, we all lined up, girls with the girls and boys with the boys, and started our march back to the school. There were three nuns in the front, three nuns in the back, and two on each side. The way they surrounded us they might as well have been prison guards. As I was walking the three blocks back to the school, my tears wouldn't stop. That was until the nun, the mean one that Rick told me he had seen with Charlie, saw me crying.

"What are you crying for," she snapped, "Charlie's gone to Heaven now. Forget about him."

I stifled my cries, but I couldn't stifle my sadness. It hung over me like a dark cloud. I felt really sad for a month – that's an eternity for a young kid. I just couldn't believe that he was actually gone. I wanted to leave that place.

6

Runaway

I TRIED TO LEAVE. In truth, a lot of kids did. I was nine years old the first time I ran away. My house was only four blocks from the school and I, quite simply, walked to my house. Before I knew it, the RCMP were knocking on my door. Nobody was home at the time, so I was totally defenceless.

"Come on," they barked as they pulled out a set of child-sized handcuffs. With me cuffed, they escorted me to the squad car and put me in the back seat like I was a criminal. They drove me back to the school and, still in handcuffs, I was walked into the classroom with all the other kids watching. It felt degrading to be in handcuffs, but once the kids saw you, you kind of felt like a hero. At least that's what I told myself. After the police took off the handcuffs, Mother Michaela made me kneel in front of the class, just like the Musqueam brothers. I got a real good strapping later on. I knew that if I ever tried to escape again, I would need a better plan to evade the long arm of the RCMP. Some accomplices might help too.

The second time I ran away, the plan was more elaborate. For starters, I wasn't doing it by myself; I had my cousins Verne and Patty, who were also students at St. Paul's, with me. Secondly, I was twelve years old this time around and had the wisdom of the last three years. Verne was from Upper Squamish, the area that my mom was now living in, which made him a real asset. Our plan was that we would sneak off the school grounds, hop a westbound train, and make our way to my mother's place once we arrived in Squamish. In the morning, we made it off the school grounds and down to the train tracks. We hopped on the first westbound train we saw and ended up in a coal car. Not helping matters, it was November, which meant it was snowy, wet, and cold. By the time we got off the train in Squamish, we were covered from head to toe in black soot and soaked to the bone. When we got to my mom's house, she couldn't even make out who we were at first because of our coal-dust disguise. That night she bathed us, cooked for us, and washed and hung our clothes. I thought for a minute that we'd actually gotten away, but in the morning, we were woken by a loud knock on the door. My mom opened the door and a big hulking RCMP officer brushed right past her. The guy must have been three hundred pounds. He pointed at us and said, "Get up! Let's go."

"Can I at least feed them?" my mom asked.

"No," croaked the cop.

But after we got dressed, before we left, my mom quietly passed me a bag full of her freshly made bannock. When we went outside, the officer put us all into the same child-sized handcuffs I had worn three years before. Unlike the time before, he also cuffed Verne, Patty, and me to each other. He put us in the back of his car, drove us down to the train station, and marched us onto a train headed back to North Vancouver. When a big, huge cop marches three kids shackled together onto a train, people notice. Everyone on that train was staring at us. I felt so embarrassed and ashamed. I didn't look up even once. I just kept my head down; we all did.

When we got back to the school, they made us kneel in the dining hall, in front of all the boys and girls who were eating. We all got the strap that night. That was the last time that I ever tried running away. Other kids still tried, mostly to no avail.

There was a time when my uncle Willard and brother Andy tried. They, like most everybody else, were quickly caught by the RCMP. One day, not long after their failed attempt, we were in the grades 1, 2, and 3 classroom when Mother Michaela came in. "Andrew, come with me," she said. Andy followed her out of the classroom, and they made their way upstairs. I had no idea what was going on, so I spotted them about a minute's time and then snuck up the same set of stairs behind them. From what I could tell, they were in the older boys' dormitory. When I peeked around the corner, I could see my brother half-naked, lying on a bed on his stomach. Mother Michaela had taken her strap off her hip and started whacking him across his bare bum. We all knew what getting strapped was by this time, and in this particular instance, Andy was getting a real bad strapping. He was bouncing around everywhere. He looked like a fish out of water. She just kept hitting him all the while telling him to "move his hands." And then Andy saw me. He stared at me. I couldn't take my eyes off him. He never made a sound, even though he was flopping around. He never cried or screamed. When she was beating him, you could see the skin, the blood, flying off with each whack. When Mother Michaela was satisfied, she wiped the blood off her strap with a cloth that she had brought with her, put it back on her hip, and walked out of the room. Her hooded robe prevented her from seeing me leaning against the wall right outside the doorway. I hated her so much. All I wanted to do was grab her and push her down the stairs. But I didn't. My fear was stronger. With Andy still lying on the bed, reeling from his injuries, I quietly made my way back downstairs. I was boiling inside.

Hate is all I ever felt for the nuns. I felt hate for the nuns because they felt hate for us. We were children witnessing trauma twenty to thirty times a day. We saw kids as young as three and four getting beat up. Lots of the kids didn't understand what was happening to them or why. Some of the kids couldn't even speak English. They would get beat up for speaking their language. Not to mention that we were constantly called ugly, stupid, savages, and dumb Indians – things like that. That's how they talked to us. Even when the nuns spoke to each other in French, we knew they were talking about us because they would say "savage" or some other slur. That's just how it was. It got a little bit easier for me when I got up to grade 4 or 5 because I learned how to become invisible. I would sit behind bigger kids, or just do whatever I had to do to not be noticed by the nuns.

7

I Tried to Be Invisible

SOME OF THE KIDS never understood, the way I did, the importance of remaining unseen. One day while in line, waiting to sit for breakfast, a kid named Louie walked up to us with a big smile on his face and two pieces of buttered toast in his hands. We all knew that he had taken the toast out of the staff dining room. Suddenly, the nun, who had had her back turned, locked eyes on Louie, ran over, snatched the toast, and smacked him on the head a couple of times. She then told him to get back in line. Louie did as he was told, and we all watched as the nun threw the perfectly good toast into the garbage. We filed into the dining hall and took our seats soon after. Unfortunately for Louie, the worst was yet to come.

As we all sat waiting for the older girls to make their rounds with the food cart, Mother Michaela walked into the hall. CRACK! – her pointer stick smacked the table. Everyone turned toward her.

"Louie, come here," she ordered. Poor Louie stood up, crying and looking really scared. He walked over and, with his head down, took his place beside her. "Louie got caught stealing. Stealing from the nuns and the priests," she decreed through her French accent. "We are a big part of the church, and if you steal from us, you are stealing from the church. And if you steal from the church you are going to Hell. Louie got caught stealing from the church and he has to be punished." She then grabbed Louie by the arm and led him to the adjacent kitchen. Out of sight from us, we all heard Louie let out two screams. I didn't know much else about his punishment until after we were finished eating and my brother Andy and I went into the kitchen to do our assigned chores.

Walking into the kitchen, we both noticed a strange smell. It was different from the garbage that we were gathering to bury outside. It was the smell of burnt flesh. Unbeknownst to us at the time, the two screams we had heard from Louie earlier were in reaction to Mother Michaela burning each one of his hands on a stove element. Each hand was burned because he had stolen two pieces of toast. What's worse is how they left him. When I saw Louie later that day, he was crying and his hands were wrapped in toilet paper. The crude bandaging had been done by the older boys because the staff never treated Louie. He was like that for almost two weeks. I remember looking at him and his hands. He couldn't hold a pencil to save his life. The toilet paper was all dried and stuck to his hands and you could see the pus oozing. That was the type of abuse you got used to when you were at the school. If you questioned the nuns, the abuse just got worse. I found that out the hard way.

There was one nun at the school who used to carry around a roughly two-inch-long hatpin. She used to get a kick out of walking up behind us and poking us in the bum with the pin, and then when we jumped, she would just start laughing. When she did it to the young kids, and they would start crying, she'd say, "Oh, don't cry. It doesn't even hurt." I remember that these unprovoked attacks went on for some time. I was one of her ten-odd favourites who she used to poke all the time. After being poked one time, I finally snapped and decided that I had had enough. I took my complaint to Mother Michaela. I explained exactly what the nun had been doing and that I was frustrated because I didn't understand what had happened for me to deserve the mistreatment. Her response after hearing me out was to go and grab the same nun that I was speaking about. As the two nuns stood over me, Mother Michaela instructed me to tell the nun exactly what I had just told her. I looked up at the nun who had been abusing me. She was glaring at me in a way that let me know she was going to get me later. I said nothing. Mother Michaela told me to leave the room.

Three nights later, that same nun came to my bed in the middle of the night. Before I knew it, I was being dragged by my pyjamas into some other room. I was totally disoriented. I figured out the nun's identity just as she started her assault. In the hall in front of her room, she began to punch me. I was very scared and in a great deal of pain, but I was determined not to let it show, not to give her the satisfaction of knowing that it hurt. This became our nightly tradition. No matter how hard or how many times I prayed to their god, he didn't answer. The beatings got so bad that I woke up on my bed one time with a blood-soaked pillow. The blood was coming from my right ear, and, since that day, I have been completely deaf in that ear. I have no recollection of going back to my bed after the beating that left me permanently deaf. I believe that I was knocked unconscious and put back into bed. I believe I was left for dead.

My job at St. Paul's was laundry. A group of us boys did laundry every Friday, and we had to work with Mother Michaela. Strangely, she was nice to work with when we did laundry. You always knew the toughness or meanness could come out, but when we did chores, I saw a gentler side of her. She'd talk while we worked; she was almost friendly, and at ten in the morning, she'd bring us for a treat of tea and toast and talk some more. No one got beaten while we did the laundry. We had about four washing machines – the old kind where you had to wring out the clothes – we washed the boys' and the girls' clothes. There were two big stoves with kettles full of water. We had to make a fire beneath the stove in order to have hot water. It was in the laundry that I became the firekeeper. Someone had to keep the fire going, and Mother Michaela didn't pick anyone for the job, so I did it because I wanted to do it. On Thursdays, boys would chop wood and pile it up high, and on Fridays I was the firekeeper.

One day when I was about twelve years old – Andy was about fourteen – we were out in the yard sitting on a swing and talking. I don't remember any other kids being out, just us. It must have been after school and before supper, between three and five o'clock. A nun – I don't remember which one – came out the door and told us to come with her. We followed her to the garden where they grew veggies like peas, and there were also pear trees and apple trees. The shovels were already there, and she told us to dig a hole.

I don't think she'd marked it off, but we must have had instructions because we dug about four or five feet long, about a foot or two wide, and about three feet deep. A rectangle. The soil was soft in the garden; it probably only took fifteen or twenty minutes. The nun stood right there and watched us. When we were digging, Andy looked up at her and asked her what the hole was for. She just said, "Garbage." She said it angrily.

At the time, it seemed strange, but we never thought anything of it. Today I'm trying not to suspect it was a grave. I don't know. I just hope it wasn't. No boys went missing then. I don't know about the girls. I once tried to talk to Andy about it, and he got angry and told me to eff off. He didn't want to talk about it, and in his eyes you could see he was hurting. You could see the pain there. He said, "I don't effing want to talk about it. Just eff off." And eff off meant change the subject. I believe that, like many of us, he's still packing the pain and the effects of residential school.

One night, not much later, an older boy woke me. His name was Steve. There were three of us. I don't know why Steve picked me: I wasn't close to him or anything. He woke me up and told me to be quiet. There was another boy with us who had forced his way into Mother Michaela's room. We went in there and I still didn't know what was going on. The door didn't look like it was forced, and I didn't know how they opened it because she did lock the door. All the nuns did.

In her room, there was a little dresser. Steve opened up the dresser drawer and it was full of candy. There were about three drawers full of things like jelly beans, jawbreakers, and gummy bears. She had all that because the nuns would sell us candy. Sometimes our parents would give us money, or they'd give money to the nuns for the candy.

We filled our pyjamas and our shirts with candy. I hid it all under my bed, under my blanket. There must have been chocolate, too, because I remember it melted. The nuns never found out about what we did, or at least we didn't hear about it. I shared my candy with my brother. You had to be very careful with the candy or the nuns would know who stole it.

When we were in Mother Michaela's room, I looked around and under the bed you could see a metal trunk. I pulled it out from under the bed. It had two handles on it and it wasn't locked. I opened it up and it was filled with money – bills. It was filled almost to the top.

I called Stevie over to look and he said, "Holy shit!" He closed the trunk and pushed it back under the bed and we kept on grabbing candy, but I'd never seen that much money in my life. The most I'd ever seen was fifteen or twenty dollars.

I was stunned. It was like finding buried treasure. I don't know where she got all that money. At the time, parents would get family allowance from the government, so maybe the family allowance went to the nuns. And the government probably sent them money for food for us. Maybe she used some of it for their food. The nuns ate normal food. Stevie told us not to tell anyone. I only started telling people about the trunk after the school closed down.

Neglect and malnourishment were commonplace. I can remember when I became really sick and developed these scabs all over my body. Finally, after I was sick for quite some time, Mother Michaela took me down to see a doctor. He said that I was malnourished and suffering from a vitamin deficiency. To treat the sores, I was to be given a special medicine, and a nun had to give me a bath every night. Every time she bathed me, she would let me know what she thought of me. She would tell me how ugly and dirty I was and how much she didn't want to touch me. I knew how gross I looked, but her sharing it with me made me feel that much worse. There was a cream that she was to put on me every night, but the only place she would put it on was my back. She made me put it on everywhere else. It was probably for the better because when she bathed me and put the cream on, she was really rough. So rough, in fact, that it would make me cry. She had no gentleness in her touch. She had no compassion for me at all. The condition I was in was bad enough. Medical treatment shouldn't make you feel worse.

I wish I could say that my permanent hearing loss or the rough baths I got were the worst things that happened to me at St. Paul's, but they weren't. The most evil thing happened to me when I was thirteen years old, just after I moved into the big boys' dormitory. The dormitory was laid out in a way that was very similar to the young boys' dormitory. There were rows of white cots, and at the end of the room a nun's bedroom with a curtained window. One night, a boy older than me – I think maybe fifteen or sixteen – vanished from the school. I don't know if he ran away, but I do know that he never came back. The nun whose bedroom was at the end of our room instructed me to take the disappeared boy's bed. It was the bed that was closest to her room. I thought it was an odd request, but I followed the nun's instruction. Nothing seemed at all different until that same nun revealed her true reason for getting me to change beds.

She woke me out of a dead sleep in the dead of night. I was slightly disoriented and foggy from having just woken up to the sister tapping me on the shoulder. When I opened my eyes, I saw the nun motioning for me to follow her into her room. I didn't understand what was going on. I scanned the dormitory looking for any clue as to why I was being asked to do what I was doing. Once we were in her room, she closed the door and told me to get in her bed. Then she sexually molested me. She continued to molest me for two years. I was her plaything. She did whatever she wanted to do to me. One thing that struck me about the whole ordeal was that everything she was doing to me she and all the other nuns said you would go to Hell for. And she was so dismissive about it. After she was finished with me, she'd say, "Go on, get out of here. And don't tell anybody." I was so ashamed and embarrassed. I felt ugly, dirty, and used. That was why I didn't want to tell anybody. Not to mention, who was I going to talk to at the school?

And I didn't tell anybody for a really long time. Apart from my drug and alcohol counsellor, the first time I really brought it up was in 2008 at the Independent Assessment Process testimonies. That doesn't mean that it didn't show, though. Instead of sadness, it came out as anger; instead of being hurt, I would choose to be mad. I held it all in. I became violent. I started fighting a lot. Every time I would talk with the nuns, I would tell them to "Fuck off." I remember Mother Michaela bringing me into her office and asking me, "What is wrong with you?"

"Fuck off," I snarled back. That was all I had to say to any of them.

8

Finding Ways to Feel Good

I WAS ONLY ABOUT thirteen and still at St. Paul's when I began to drink. During the weekends we spent at home, drinking became a way of life. My friends did it, so I followed them. Sometimes we got to come home on Fridays or Saturdays and we'd go back to the school around five o'clock on Sundays. Fridays and Saturdays were for drinking. There used to be more bushes on the reserve; there was a place down the street that had big round drainpipes – culverts – and we'd climb in and that's where we'd drink on weekends. Then we went to church on Sunday mornings. Sometimes I'd be hungover. Church was just another place I had to be. I didn't actually go to save my soul. Today I don't like church. I have nothing to do with it.

In them days, a case of beer cost $2.25 or something, so me and my friends would put our money together and we'd go stand outside the nearby pub and we'd say, "Hey, mister, can you get us some booze?" Or we'd stand beside the liquor store – it was cheaper at the store – and we'd ask someone to buy us booze. Someone always would. One time a guy tried to run off with the booze he'd bought with our money, but we chased him, so he turned around and came back. He didn't want anyone to know that he was supplying us with alcohol.

Sometimes we'd go looking for booze in the cars in the parking lot of the nearby pub, and we'd try a car door. In them days, the car doors had a little fly window, and we'd just go like that – bang – and we'd bend it open, get our hand inside, and open the car door.

Once we put our money together, we'd get three or four cases of beer, and we'd all sit around somewhere and drink. Sometimes we'd go to someone's parents' place – some of the guys had record players – and we'd sit and talk and listen to rock 'n' roll: Duane Eddy, Chuck Berry, Fats Domino, Buddy Holly, Ritchie Valens. I didn't really care for Elvis.

We'd drink to get drunk, to feel good. Sometimes, though, we'd drink and the anger would surface. You'd think about the school, and you'd get angry at someone. It wasn't about them. It had nothing to do with them at all. For me, I'd get angry because of my guilt and my suffering. I'd think about being sexually abused and I'd start arguing or fighting with a friend – whoever I was with at the time – but it had nothing to do with them at all.

During the summers, we'd be home during June, July, and August. The summers were happy times. If ever the guys fought, the next day we'd be okay again. We also drank a lot in the summers, especially on Fridays and Saturdays. Those were our party days.

A lot of times, we'd hang out and listen to music or go down to the beach and go swimming. Sometimes the girls our age would come with us. Other times, we'd jump on the ferry and go to a movie on Hastings. Or if we wanted to go to what we'd call the Big Time Movies, we'd walk to the ones on Granville. I think you had to pay a nickel more. On Hastings, there was the Lux, the Odeon, and the Rex, and a movie there was fifteen cents, but if we walked up to Granville – to the Orpheum – it'd be twenty cents.

There also used to be a drive-in and a whole bunch of us used to go sit on the fence outside. We had to climb the fence and sort of squat on there to watch the movie. Somebody would jump down and turn up all the speakers so we could hear. The drive-in was about a mile from the reserve, and we'd walk along the tracks to get there, then we'd sneak under the screen to get to the other side. If someone had money, they'd jump down from the fence and go get some popcorn, and they'd pass it around. We thought nothing of it. At eleven or twelve o'clock the movie would end and we'd walk back home in the night.

During those summers, my mom had taken my two sisters with her to Upper Squamish, so it was just me and my brother Andy at home, and often we wouldn't see my dad for a long time. A lot of times when we went downtown, we'd go alone at three or four in the morning and that's when we'd do B and Es. We'd steal food because we were hungry. There used to be a bakery near the reserve, and a grocery store. Sometimes we'd break in at night; someone would kick down the door and we'd load up with food. There was also a Safeway that we'd break into, and we'd steal bologna or ham. As long as it wasn't too big, we could stick things under our shirts.

Our dad was often in Vancouver; I suspect he was drinking. He'd be away for days or weeks at a time. When he came home, it was like a guilt trip for him, and he'd get us pork chops or steak and he'd cook them. He'd cook us a real good meal and buy us lots of bread.

When I was with my friends on weekends and during the summer, we'd never talk about the school. It was just good to be away from it. If we did talk about the school, we'd talk about a nun and say things like "that effing nun," or "effing Sister."

Mostly it was silent between us. We all witnessed the verbal and physical abuse, yet I thought I was the only one being sexually abused. Now I think others probably were too. My bed was near the nun's room, and there were two other beds nearby that belonged to other boys around my age. They're both dead now. One of those boys – he was one of my best buddies – sometimes, when we got drunk, for seemingly no reason he would start to cry. He wouldn't talk; he'd just cry. He was hurting, and we never knew why. We always thought it was about a girl, but he didn't even have a girl. We just knew if he got drunk, he might cry, and we'd carry on doing our thing and let him cry. When we drank, I felt like doing what my friend did, but I never did. For me, the pain and hurt came out in anger. When my buddy cried, nobody even asked him what was wrong, but we all knew what was going on at the school. We left there on Fridays and Saturdays for a reason. We left to forget everything that happened during the week.

When I left St. Paul's in 1959, they gave me some kind of report on my personality. It said I was "violent and incorrigible." The feeling was mutual. In fact, the last thing I ever said to Mother Michaela was "fuck off." All the students and staff knew that the school was shutting down at the end of the 1959 school year. It had been condemned and was scheduled to be torn down. Despite this knowledge, the nuns still made all of us students clean the school until it was spotless. It was on one of those final days, on hands and knees scrubbing the floor, that I finally decided for myself that I was done. What we were doing made no sense at all, and with the school shutting down for good, I knew no one was going to come after me. I took the pillowcase off the pillow on my bed, stuffed it with all my belongings, threw it out a fire exit, and then left out the same fire exit. When Mother Michaela saw me walking away, she shouted out to me.

"Where do you think you're going? Get back here."

"Fuck off," I said to her, without looking back or breaking stride.

After that day, St. Paul's was in my past, but the invisible wounds it had cut ran deep, so deep that I had to hit rock bottom before I realized the severity of those wounds.

Whenever people ask me what I learned at that school, my answer remains the same: I learned how to steal, I learned how to lie, I learned how to mistrust, and I learned how to hate. I stole because I was hungry. I lied because I knew that the truth didn't matter. I learned how to mistrust because none of them at that school trusted me. And I hated because it was all I could do. I hated the nuns, I hated the priests, I hated the policemen, I hated the judges, I hated government officials, and I hated the teachers. As far as I was concerned, I hated everyone. And for all of it I owe thanks to my time at St. Paul's Indian Residential School.

9

On Our Own

WHEN I LEFT THE school for good in 1959, I was fourteen
going on fifteen years old and filled with pent-up anger.
We – my brother Andy and I – moved back into our home,
four blocks away from the school. Of course, by now, our
childhood home was quite a bit different than it was when
we left for St. Paul's. Since the school was slated to be
demolished, my mom had taken my two sisters and Ross
up to Squamish for good to live with her, and my dad wasn't
dealing with any of it very well. He was drinking a lot. It
was easy to tell he was because the booze would make him
come unglued. He was usually a pretty stoic guy, but when
he was drinking, he would cry and hug us a lot. Because he
was in a bad way, it was essentially Andy and me living by
ourselves: a sixteen-year-old and his fourteen-year-old kid
brother.

The summer after we left the school, a bunch of us signed
up to go to the big cadet camp in Vernon. The week before
we were supposed to leave, my Papa passed away. I went and
talked with my Ta'ah and asked her if I should stick around
for his funeral. She told me that I should go and that I could
say my goodbyes before I left. I remember seeing my Papa's
coffin and knowing that he was inside. I said my goodbyes

to him. The very next morning, my Ta'ah sent me off to the train with a big hug.

After six weeks in Vernon, a bunch of us boarded the train back to North Vancouver. When we were pulling up to our destination, we saw the thing all of us wanted to see more than anything: up on the hill, there was a big grader ripping the roof off St. Paul's. When we got off the train, a bunch of us made off to watch the school get demolished. That day, I saw two nuns packing that trunk I'd seen under Mother Michaela's bed. They were moving out. I was standing around and all of a sudden I saw them with that trunk. One had one handle and the other held the other. They were taking it to the convent. When the residential school shut down, they gave the nuns a choice: either they could leave the nunnery or they could stay. About six nuns left and they bought a house on Fraser Street. I heard a rumour that they paid cash for it. There's still one nun left there.

I was happy the school was gone, but unfortunately it still lived inside many of us. It certainly did in me.

Getting back home from cadet camp, we did the best we could. Andy took care of me a lot. He would do most of the cooking. Our Ta'ah would come over to do our laundry for us. My relationship with my Ta'ah was different, but not on her end. I was too full of anger to be connected to her in the same way that I was before residential school. With little to no guidance, we were free to roam. There were a bunch of us like that on the reserve. Most of our parents were in the same boat. It seemed like most of our parents couldn't take it when we were at St. Paul's. I didn't really think about how hard it must have been for them. Rather, we would just hang out and walk around. There were about twenty of us boys who would get together every day and night and get into something. None of us had any money to buy food or anything like that, so we kept on stealing whatever we could get our hands on: bread, bologna, mustard, peanut butter, jam – you name it, we'd eat it. It wasn't long before us young guys got into a lot more trouble.

One night, coming home from a day of hanging out with the gang, I found Andy at home dancing around and acting drunk. He'd found one of my dad's booze stashes and had started to drink it. We'd never drunk from our dad's booze before. Finding it was a thrill.

"Come on, can I have some?" I kept asking him.

"No," he'd answer. He wouldn't budge. Sensing that he had put his foot down, I decided to go on my own search of our house to find another one of my dad's hiding spots. When I found the bottle of rum, I popped the top off and started drinking. After that, I brought it to all the guys my age in my gang. I already knew the booze brought up a lot of things inside of me that I didn't like. Of course, when you're that young, you don't really understand how seriously and fast something can get out of control. This was especially true now that we didn't even have the structure of school.

After residential school, I felt unloved. In school, the nuns would say I was ugly or dumb, so I didn't feel good about myself. I always felt like I wasn't good enough. That's why I drank a lot in the first place. I was always getting in trouble back then. I didn't like it, but it was compulsive. I would do things and not think, *This could make me go to jail.* I didn't have good self-esteem or a good sense of myself, so it didn't matter what I did. I just did what everyone else – the other guys – did. In a way, getting into trouble felt inevitable.

Soon enough, drinking became our priority. Imagine a bunch of kids, fresh out of residential school, with their families gone and nothing to do. We spent a lot of time looking for trouble. I started fighting a lot. It wasn't until my anger got the better of me that I really thought I had a problem.

One night, at a party, I was getting into it with somebody, and we were getting ready to fight. My brother Andy, as he often did, attempted to break it up. He was my protector. I think Andy and I fought that night because we'd both been drinking and because were both interested in the same girl, and she was going from me to him and from him to me and we both didn't like it. We'd fought a couple times before – fist fights – but something was different that night. I wasn't going to take no for an answer from anyone. I had a knife on me. I turned on Andy. I stabbed my brother and slashed him up really bad. I slashed his face up and everything. I almost killed him.

After we fought, I don't know who called the cops, but they came. By then we were broken up. Andy went to the hospital. I later learned he got something like five hundred stitches in his face, arms, chest, and hands. I hid in the bush and watched the police look for me. They were all over.

I was on the run for a few hours. Of course, I had no place to go. I couldn't go home. I was hiding and I was watching these cops with rifles strapped to their shoulders walking around looking for me. Thankfully, they didn't have dogs back in them days. Sometimes they'd be so close to me that if I'd reached out of the bush, I would have been able to touch them. But they were persistent – they knew I was somewhere around there. I was walking down a gravel road and there was a cop walking toward me. He had a rifle. He looked at me and I looked at him and I ran. He yelled at me to stop, but I kept running. I ran by the house, and then I tripped and fell down. I believe this is when I lost my glasses. I could have gotten up. I could have got away, but I thought, *Where am I going to go?* I lay there and I finally let them catch me. The cop picked me up and cuffed my arms behind my back and brought me to the police station. At fifteen, I was back in handcuffs, this time set to be charged with attempted manslaughter. I remember all the police kept staring at me. I think they couldn't believe what I'd done to my family.

Now I think my anger at my brother when we fought that night had something to do with St. Paul's. Everything just came out.

I spent that weekend in a cell at the police station. On Monday I went to court, and they remanded me into custody. I was only in court for about five minutes. They recommended I get a lawyer to defend myself, but I knew what I'd done. They knew it too. The clothes I had on still had my brother's blood all over them.

10

Oakalla

THAT SAME DAY, the police brought me to the Oakalla Prison Farm in Burnaby. I remember two policemen handcuffed me again and put me in the back of a car. I'd heard of Oakalla. Some of the guys I knew had gone there.

I remember the officers bringing me up the steps and banging three times on a knocker. A little window opened, and the guard looked out, said, "Prisoner coming in!" and slammed the window closed. Then he opened the door; it was metal and there were bars on the door. He let me in, and I remember – I'll never forget – the sound of the door slamming. Metal hitting metal. The police brought me inside, signed some papers, and Oakalla took over. They asked me my name and my birthday. I'm sure I was the youngest one there. I waited in a holding cell, where they brought me my dinner on a tray. They took all my clothes and searched me. You had to spread your legs and bend over. They were looking for drugs, heroin especially. They brought me my prison garb and blankets and a pillowcase. In my cell, there was a toilet beside the bed and a sink, and that was it. I remember the bars on the door and that there was hardly any walking space in the cell. They'd put me in semi-max; it was full of people waiting for sentencing from all across BC – the worst of the worst. There were pedophiles, murderers – all of them waiting for their trial.

If St. Paul's prepared me for anything, it was prison. I was fully institutionalized. At Oakalla, you were locked up for twenty-two hours a day. Besides the two hours you got out in the yard every day at two o'clock, the only time you were out of your cell was for meals. I thought I was pretty tough when I went in there. I wasn't. I was a scrawny little fifteen-year-old kid. I'd watch all these older guys out in the yard fighting. These guys were really big, and they were all crazy. *Holy cow, fuck that,* I would think to myself. I was scared more than anything else. Every night, back in my cell, I would cry. Never loudly – you didn't want anyone else to hear. You had to be pretty tough at Oakalla, but every night, I would bury my head in my pillow and cry.

When I got to Oakalla, I was already conditioned not to show my feelings. You could be happy or angry, but you always had to act tough. I knew that. If someone looked at you, you'd say, "What the eff are you looking at?" It was very dysfunctional, but from being in residential school I was already like that. I also knew that when someone's abusing you, you just look at them and don't cry. Just stare at them, no matter what they do to you. That's what it meant to be institutionalized.

All those of us who'd been in residential school – most of us Natives had – were like that. The things the other guys did – their crimes – came from anger and from drinking too. I'm not making excuses, but it all stemmed from being abused at residential school. Some guys who were abused would turn around and abuse other people, even girls.

There was no place to hide in there. Everywhere you went, you were in the view of the guards. In the yard, there was a guard with a rifle on top of the wall in each corner. Early on in my time there, I kept to myself. There was a really friendly guard in there who started talking to me. For three days all I did was talk to the guy. He'd ask me about myself – my name, where I was from, stuff like that.

Then one day these two Native guys came over, leaned on the wall, and started chatting me up. They asked me similar questions to the guard's and wanted to know what I was in there for. After a few minutes they asked me to follow them. They took me to an area of the yard where all the Indians hung out. They called it the West Wing. I was badly near-sighted so my glasses were as thick as a Coke bottle, but I'd lost them before I went to prison, when I was on the run. These guys knew I could not see very well and took the time to introduce me to the two hundred other Indians locked up there. Most guys, including myself, were in there waiting for trial. From that time on, while I was in Oakalla, I spent my time with those guys.

I told the other Natives what I'd done to my brother, and they brought me to see the jailhouse lawyer. There were always jailhouse lawyers. He told me to say that my brother was a big bully and he beat me all the time, but I wouldn't say that because it wasn't true. I felt terrible for what I did.

For the two hours that we spent out in the yard every day, we would play cards and smoke cigarettes. The older guys looked out for me. They'd roll my cigarettes and everything. We'd also find each other at church every Sunday. It turned out there were a lot of guys from St. Paul's at Oakalla. The socializing in the yard and at church, though enjoyable, did little to hide how terrible that place truly was.

At night, you could hear inmates getting sexually molested by other inmates. You could hear them crying and the guys molesting them telling them to shut up. You could also tell when a guy was committing suicide. That was because the only way they could do it was to tie their shirt around the bars in their cell door. Everybody on the range would get real quiet and listen as the guy choked and kicked his feet against the bars. Nobody ever called for the guards. The guards would make their rounds every hour or two and you could hear them yell when they would find a dead inmate. They didn't even cut the shirt off their necks; you would see the guy roll by on a gurney with the shirt still snared around their neck. There was also a death row at Oakalla and, though I never witnessed it, I know they used to execute prisoners by hanging them in the elevator shaft. It was a pretty grim place.

At least the Native guys took care of me. We stuck together. Some of them you didn't trust, but the other guys protected me, even from other Natives who were going to the pen. They'd tell those guys to leave me alone. Some guys would try to make friends with you for a reason; a lot of guys got raped in there – younger guys. I got warned.

One time, I got a new cellmate. He was an older white guy, probably in his forties. He tried to sexually assault me. I was going to sleep and he came over and lay down beside me. He put his penis on my leg and tried to kiss me. I pushed him away and I grabbed my metal cup and started beating on him. He started screaming and the guards came and dragged me away. I'd beat him pretty bad. He went to the hospital and I went to solitary confinement. I stayed there for a week.

Solitary at Oakalla meant being in a cell downstairs by yourself. There were about four of us down there in separate cells. The cell was regular – it had a toilet and a sink and a bed. You came out to get your meals and you'd come back with a tray and eat by yourself. You'd be allowed out for an hour, but the guards stood there and made sure you didn't talk to anyone else in solitary. Sometimes they'd give you a magazine to read, and I read them all. There was nothing else to do.

After three months in Oakalla, I went back to court for sentencing. My Ta'ah was there and so was my dad and my lawyer. I pleaded guilty. They were going to charge me with manslaughter, but they dropped it down to aggravated assault. After that, I went back to Oakalla while they wrote up a sentencing report. This time they put me in the East Wing, which was maximum security. There, they didn't even let you outside. They'd let you out for breakfast; they'd give you a tray of food downstairs and you'd bring it back up to your cell. It was the same for lunch and supper. Between breakfast and lunch, they let you out of your cell for one hour and you could congregate with everyone on your tier; then you went back to your cell.

They'd tell you on a Monday where you were going for the rest of your sentence. I was sentenced to serve seven years. Because I was only fifteen at the time, I didn't go to the New Westminster penitentiary. Rather, I served out my time at Haney Correctional Institution, out in Maple Ridge, a young man's prison.

11

Haney Correctional

AT HANEY, ALL THE inmates were between thirteen and twenty-five years of age. Of the facility's eight hundred or so inmates, I would guess that five or six hundred of them were Native. When you got there and met the other inmates, the first thing you got asked was what residential school you went to. There were about sixteen of us in there from North Vancouver, from Squamish. All of us had gone to St. Paul's. Some of my friends were in there: Patty, his brother Harold, a guy we called Cussie, Francis, Larry, Swede, Rick, Rickie, Gilbert. They all ended up at Haney. We all knew that sooner or later we'd end up at Haney. Everyone knew that you disappeared, went to court, and disappeared again. It was common: St. Paul's, then Haney. I think one of the guys burned a church down. I don't remember what the rest did to end up there. A couple of them were violent, or stole cars, or broke into stores. Most of the guys committed their crimes while they were drunk. It was just how it was. At least at Haney they tried to give us something. They tried to rehabilitate us.

When I arrived at Haney, there was a big tournament going on. I was in my cell in Unit 6 when one of the guards came and asked for floor hockey players. I didn't have a clue about floor hockey, but I thought, *Okay, I'll go.* I liked sports. Floor hockey jail-style is pretty rough. We were flying all over the place. You had to learn pretty quick.

Haney had a better atmosphere than Oakalla, but you still had to have that tough-guy thing – you know, *Don't mess with me.* You had to adopt that style. The attitude was you don't like the guards, you don't like your counsellor, you don't like anybody in authority. Everybody felt that way.

At Haney, we were in a dorm with about forty guys. They mixed us. They put the Natives with the whites. There was just one Asian there in all the years I was there. There were a couple of Black guys. The dorm had single beds, not bunk beds. You had a locker that you could put your belongings in. There was a table you could pull out if you wanted to write a letter home.

School was good at Haney. It was all male teachers. We picked on one of the teachers and he'd say "Eff you guys!" and go stomping out, saying he was going to quit. The principal would have to convince him to come back, and he'd have to tell us to leave the teacher alone. We took English, science, math, and social studies. There were about twenty guys in a class. I took it seriously. I was in school for about a year; I got to grade 9.

At first my studies went well. I did my homework, and when I needed help I'd go ask someone in my unit who was smarter than me. There were some pretty educated people in there. I liked algebra; I got really good at it. Residential school had taught me what to do. I listened, did well in my classes, and even attended a rehabilitation centre – my first rehab visit – while I was in there.

At Haney I also did arts and crafts like copper work. I started to make a guitar, but I didn't finish it. I took training in painting – interiors and exteriors. I had only one unit to go – spray painting – before I was finished the course, but being a dumb, young kid, I got mad at the teacher and walked out. Still, when I took painting, I got into it. We painted the dining room where the inmates ate. I remember I was painting the bars for the guys' cells when JFK got shot. We were listening to music on the radio, and they broke off and announced that he got shot. We all just looked at each other and said, *Holy cow.*

I was at Haney for about eighteen months before I was paroled and went to live with my mom in Squamish. I went to Howe Sound Secondary for about six months, but I got sent back to Haney when I breached the conditions of my parole. I don't remember exactly what I did, but I probably got drunk back on the reserve one weekend.

Once I was back at Haney after my first time being paroled, I was no longer in school because I'd been paroled and reincarcerated. So they sent me out to slash bush. They'd bring us up a mountain in a big truck. They gave us rain gear and told us that if we wanted to run away, we could go ahead – and then they left us out there on the side of the mountain. We slashed bush all day in the cold. It was winter. Sometimes we'd make a fire and make coffee over it while we shivered. They'd finally come and get us at four o'clock. They only let guys like me – guys they knew wouldn't kill each other – clear bush like that. After being reincarcerated, I served the rest of my time in the same way I had been serving the first part. I made sure not to stir the pot.

That was my pattern: I got paroled and sent back to Haney three times. One time I was only out for four days. I remember one time I was in the holding cell and my teacher passed me. He was so happy I was getting out. But when I told him I was coming back, he just walked away from me.

Another time when I was out, I went after a guy with a rifle. That time I got another year added to my sentence. I was around nineteen or twenty by then. There was a party on the reserve, and at the party was a guy who had beaten up one of my friends, made his nose bleed. A group of us – me and my friends – were down at the beach drinking and we decided to go after that guy. I stopped at home and got my dad's old rifle. I went after him with it. That rifle didn't work. We never even had bullets for it. And the guy we were after didn't even come out from the party. Still, I was sent back to Haney for assault with a weapon. Just the fact that I had a rifle got me sent back.

At Oakalla there had been a lot of anger. There were suicides, and inmates on death row. Haney had none of that. It was better, but it was still jail. In some ways, it felt like an extension of residential school, but it was actually better. We ate normal food at Haney because there were inmates learning to cook.

One time at Haney I got in trouble because I wrote a letter to my sister Bea and in it I said I liked it there. The guards read your mail, so I got in trouble for that. You're not supposed to like jail. So the guards started getting me up at six o'clock in the morning and I had to go out and mop the walls and the floors as punishment. After supper, everyone else would play basketball or do arts and crafts, and there I was mopping the halls. Eventually, they asked me if I still liked it there and I said no. The punishment ended then.

I was also punished twice for fighting and was put in the hole (solitary confinement). One time, three of us jumped a guy who was picking on my friend and beat him up. I went to the hole for thirty days. Another time, I was sent there for five days, also for fighting.

The hole was a dark cell with just a little hole or a slot in the door so the guard could look at you. There was no light. It was about four or five feet wide, maybe six or seven feet long, and about eight feet high. It was all tile. Tile on the ceiling, the floor, the walls. I think that's how I survived, by counting the tiles. There wasn't even a bed. I just had one blanket that I'd sleep with on the floor. Food was five or six pieces of bread and water that the guards would bring you once a day. They'd watch you eat it. It was hard because the hole was above the kitchen, so you could smell the cooking. You could always tell when someone got out of the hole because their faces would be so pale.

Sometimes, on weekends, my dad, my sister, and my oldest brother, Ross, came to see me. Andy came once, but it was uncomfortable because he was still all scarred. They didn't come that often – not even once a month – because they had to catch a bus and then take a taxi. It was a long way for them to come and visit.

I remember the day I left Haney. You had to go down a real long road. I remember the first time I left, I looked back and felt sad to go: I had been sort of glad to be there. I had almost killed my brother, so I deserved it. But the last time I went down that road, in 1964, I made up my mind that I wasn't going back. I ended up serving four and a half years of my seven-year sentence. My mostly exemplary behaviour inside prison didn't translate to good behaviour outside, though. I think Haney gave us young guys a good opportunity to straighten out. I could have taken mechanics, carpentry, or drafting, but I didn't. My past still haunted me. My past still dictated my future.

12

Longshoreman

I GOT OUT OF PRISON in 1964 and, like I said, I hadn't learned anything. I remember having nowhere to go and making my way back to North Van. I remember seeing Andy for the first time after getting out of prison. He hugged me and told me he forgave me for what I had done to him. It was really hard because his face was all scarred up from the knife wounds; it still is. His love did little to help me. I fell right back into my old ways: drinking and, pretty soon, drugging. It didn't help that it was the sixties, a decade where the culture of young people revolved around drug use.

At first, there were some positive things happening in my life. When I got paroled the last time, I was twenty. By that time, all my brothers had followed my dad's path and become longshoremen. I didn't really have anything much going on for work – the odd labour job – so I was interested when Andy phoned me up and said, "You should come down here. There's a lot of work. The Japanese orange shipment just came in." I made my way down to the dispatch office, but because I didn't get there until ten thirty, there was no work for me. I actually didn't end up starting until the following month.

It was January of 1965 when I got dispatched for the first time in what was to be a forty-three-year career. That first job was a memorable one too. When you first start working as a longshoreman, you get all the hard, labour-heavy jobs. Our task that day was to open up the hatches and unload the cargo. The cargo was what made that first job so memorable: it was all whisky. We would have to get down into the hatches and manually unload it. Longshoremen, especially back then, had quite the reputation for drinking. I was already a full-blown alcoholic, so I fit right in.

What we did, out of the view of the foremen, was we cracked open a few bottles, poured them in a bucket and mixed it with water. Every time anyone went down below, they would take a big glug of the Scotch and water. I was drunk as a skunk. Anytime a poor alcoholic like me could get free booze was a good time. I thought it was great. So, at least initially, that's why I stayed longshoring. And then I got my first paycheque. In them days, a good living wage was something like $1.25 an hour – I was making $3.00 an hour. It was really good money. We got paid weekly, so every week I would put away $10 from my $150 paycheque, and then I would drink the rest. At the time, I was content living paycheque to paycheque.

Back in them days, there were a lot of Squamish working as longshoremen. A lot of whites, too, but I mostly worked with the other Natives. A lot of my friends were longshoring: Timmy, Ricky, Louie, Ducky, a guy named Pogo, all my uncles. There were also a lot of Tsleil-Waututh and Musqueam, and we all mixed. A lot of them had been to residential school. Before I started longshoring, I had learned to hate white people. To me, all they represented was everything that was bad in my world. White people were the RCMP, the judges, and the nuns. Working as a longshoreman showed me that they weren't all bad. I mean, there was definitely still a lot of racism happening. Even the ones who accepted me would always be sure to remind me that I was an Indian. That was my nickname, in fact: "Indian." As bad as it sounds, it truly was a different time and environment. I don't think they meant it maliciously.

I got to work with a lot of my friends and family, actually. By the time I started working there, Andy had been there for around five years, so he was way higher up than I was. Some of the guys knew I was Ross's brother or Flossie's son. Rick and I worked together a lot, worked our way up together. The way you did it back then was you'd have to go to the dispatch hall for six o'clock in the morning. A whole bunch of us would make the same long bus trip over from North Van to the dispatch hall, which in them days was on Dunlevy Avenue, close to Oppenheimer Park. We'd all hop on a bus at a stop right by the reserve. The bus cost a quarter. The bus would stop again on the North Shore and pick up a bunch more Natives from the reserve at Capilano. The bus would take us to right by the Hudson's Bay in downtown Vancouver, and we'd catch a transfer bus to the dispatch office. There was a lot of camaraderie on those bus trips. Once you got to the hall, you would rip the top of your smoke pack off, write your name on it, and put it in a stack with all the other names. Then, in the order that their names were stacked, guys would get sent to different jobs. The longer you stayed, and the more hours you put in, the higher you moved up and the better your jobs got. Of course, because we were the young guys, we would get all the bull work. As it turns out, it was mostly because nobody else wanted to do it. We'd pack around huge sacks of coffee, cowhides, and pulp paper mostly. If you didn't pack your weight, someone would let you know. That was my routine until a few years later, when I bought my first car. It was a 1952 Chevy. I paid seventy-five dollars for it. It was a really ugly green colour, but it ran good. I missed those bus rides, but not more than I enjoyed the freedom of having my own vehicle.

Longshoring could be fun too. In the mornings there was a dispatch from seven o'clock to nine, then another around ten or eleven, and then at noon and another at three o'clock. A lot of times we'd sit around the dispatch hall and play cards. Or we'd walk up to the courthouse and listen to the cases. Sometimes on Mondays, a longshoreman we'd know would walk in – guys would get picked up on the weekend for being drunk. We all took our turn. You'd get picked up and go to court and they'd call out your name in front of everyone. All the longshoremen would cheer you on. Usually, they'd let you go with a five-dollar fine or so. It happened to me once.

When I first made longshoring, I worked down below in the ship, but eventually I got to operate the crane. There's the hatch tender who signals the crane, and the winch driver who actually operates the crane. I got to do both of those jobs.

There aren't too many Squamish men longshoring now. My son did it when he was seventeen, but his mom made him quit and go back to high school. Today there's a contract with the Port – Squamish owns Lynn Terminal – that says 33 percent of the longshoremen have to be Squamish, but they don't enforce it.[1]

Even with a career, my life began to revolve around partying. It got to be all-consuming. A lot of interesting things happen at parties.

....

1 *The Lynnterm Terminal was known by Sam and his fellow longshoremen as the Lynn Terminal.*

13

Misery Loves Company

I USED TO FALL in love a lot back then. I guess misery loves company. I was miserable, and I think – in the back of my mind, at least – I wanted people to be miserable with me. I've been married four times and engaged at least ten.

I met my first wife, the mother of my two sons, on our reserve in the early sixties. She was actually a student at St. Paul's at the same time that I was. Though we were at the school at the same time, we never really interacted with each other because we were obviously different sexes, and she was three or four years younger than I was. Anyway, we used to have these big Potlatches with canoe races on our reserve, and I saw her there with her sister. They were from a different reserve. I thought she was pretty, and she smiled at me, so I decided to walk over and chat her up. A couple of weeks passed, and I saw her again. We sparked up a conversation and started seeing each other.

I took her to a rock concert for our first date. I think it was the Beach Boys. Sometimes we went the movies. I had my first motorcycle then – a Yamaha – and I used to jump on it and ride down to see her.

I had a reputation as a heavy drinker, but she was different. She didn't drink. Not even a drop. She went to church and was really into her school work. Most of the girls drank, but she didn't. Even though we'd both gone to St. Paul's, we never talked about it, not even once. It's the same with my brothers and sisters; we never talk about what happened to us at the school. It's just a dark part of our lives.

When I proposed, we were sitting on the stairs of her house and talking. I don't think I asked her to marry me; I just pulled out the ring and showed it to her. She put it on, so I took that as an acceptance, and I felt happy. I think she did too.

I got that ring from a jewellery store across the street from Army & Navy. It was a small ring, but it cost about seven hundred dollars – in them days that was something! I think the diamond was a one-pointer.

We were engaged for a long time before we married because she was still in school. I remember going to her graduation and she was showing off her ring to all the girls, her classmates. Her grad was at a hotel down by Stanley Park. It was quite fancy. I think I rented a car for that; I felt proud of her.

Eventually, we had a big wedding at the church (St. Paul's) on the reserve. My wife had a white dress that her parents and grandpa bought for her. I rented a tuxedo; Ross and Andy did too. We had a big reception. It was a big party at her reserve; she was related to almost everyone there.

I felt good, happy, when we got married. I was excited about our life together. After we married, I gained a lot of weight. My first wife was a good cook; she'd make stews and soups, and I wasn't used to eating like that. We also went to a lot of Native events together, like dances, and there was a lot of drinking and drugging going on.

Not long after I married, I lost both my Ta'ah and my father. Ta'ah had cancer and so did my dad. He passed away four days after Ta'ah. They were in the same hospital, both of them dying of cancer in separate rooms. We'd go visit, and one of us would stay with my dad and the other would go sit with Ta'ah. I don't know how old Ta'ah was, but my dad must have been in his sixties. He'd retired from longshoring. In them days, Squamish funerals were at the church. There would be a service and then the casket would be open and everyone would walk by to say goodbye and then greet the family. Ta'ah and my dad were buried in Upper Squamish on a cold day. It was winter. I felt very sad losing them both like that. I was hurt, like everyone else in the family. My mom passed away quite a few years later; she had a heart condition and died on the operating table.

My marriage was good in the beginning. By this time, I was living in a different house, which my dad had bought. It was an old wartime house, a tiny little thing. When I got married, my dad moved out – went and lived with my sisters – and left the house for my wife and me to live in. We lived there for quite a while, too, between five and ten years. We had two boys. Even though I was a father, I was drinking a lot. Being a longshoreman didn't help any. Back then, you'd have five beers with lunch and a dozen by the time you were getting home.

Pretty soon, I started doing drugs too. At Haney, the drugs had started coming into the place in my last year there – mostly LSD – but I had never tried any. Eventually, I tried marijuana. The first time I did marijuana, we were in my car down on the beach and one of the guys asked if we wanted to smoke a joint. There were three of us guys and we all smoked and started laughing together. It felt good. Around then, there were a lot of parties to go to, and all of them had drugs.

A good story I have from back then happened at a party on my reserve sometime in the mid- to late sixties. Back in them days we used to hang out with these two Black guys all the time. Both of them were longshoremen as well. Their names were Ron and Robert, and they were identical twins. Anyway, this one time, we were having a party, nothing really out of the ordinary. We were all hanging out having beers when Ron and Robert walked in with another guy, a guy we didn't know. Ron and Robert explained that he was a cousin of theirs who was up from Seattle to play some shows. They said he was a singer and guitar player and they were backing him up because he didn't bring his band from Seattle. The fellow was pretty quiet and kept to himself. Sensing he was lonely, I decided to go over and introduce myself.

"Hey, how's it going? My name is Sam," I said.

"Hey man, my name is Jimi. You want to smoke a joint?" he asked.

"Sure," I replied.

So we talked a little and got to smoking the joint this Jimi guy had. To this day I don't think I've ever smoked any pot that was that strong. We both stopped talking to each other. I stood there dead quiet for a couple of minutes, totally spaced out, before I spoke.

"Well, hey, it was good meeting you. I'm going to go home. Take care."

We said our goodbyes and I headed off. It wasn't until a couple months, maybe a year, later that I saw my smoking buddy on the television, and I thought, *Hey, I know that guy. He's Ron and Robert's cousin, who I met at that party.* He was getting really big. And that's my story about the time I smoked a joint with Jimi Hendrix.

Around then, I used to go down to Stanley Park with my wife. They'd have "be-ins" and we'd go down there to see all the hippies smoking drugs and drinking wine. We'd have some beers and we'd watch, but within a year we were right down there with them. Our hair was long and we were smoking marijuana.

Then the mescaline came along, then the LSD and, of course, heroin. The first time I did mescaline, I was at a be-in with my wife. I was rolling joints and this guy came along and asked if I wanted to trade for mescaline, so I traded four joints for four little pills. I didn't take them then; but later, when we were going to a rock concert, I took one. I remember sitting there getting stoned. I remember walking to the front and feeling like I was floating. I had to check to see if my legs were working. I don't remember who was playing at that concert, but it was at the PNE Forum, and I remember all the colours were flashing out at me and it felt good, and a bit scary too. Another time, I took one pill and felt nothing, so then I took four. My wife had to walk me around the reserve for a long time before she brought me home, and I crashed on the couch for hours.

I was lucky because I only did heroin a couple of times and it made me really sick. The guy who introduced me to it died of an overdose. I did just a little bit each time, but it was no good. You get a rush, but then it feels ugly. I didn't like it. I especially didn't like it after the one overdose I had. I came to in the hospital. I had no idea how long it had been since my OD. The doctors had brought me back. I remember being really emotional about the whole ordeal.

"I'm so sorry, God; I'm so sorry, God." I couldn't even pray. I just kept repeating that. The nurses had stripped me down – they cut off my shoelaces, my pants, and my shirt – and put me in a bed hooked up to the IV and all these tubes.

After a couple of hours, a doctor came in and said to me, "Mr. George, you're okay, you can go home now. You know, one of these days you're going to come in here and we're not going to be able to help you. We're going to have to let you go."

"I know," is all I could muster. I left the hospital and went back to the same drug house that I had OD'd at. I was in a bad way.

At first, I only did drugs on weekends and got my supply of marijuana from guys on the reserve. After a while, I started selling drugs: marijuana, mescaline, acid. This was in my hippie years. I'd sell to whoever came to the house – mostly people from around the reserve. I wasn't afraid of going back to prison. I was never caught. I never even thought about getting caught. I didn't make much money from selling drugs. I'd sell a nickel bag for five dollars or a dime bag for ten. I got the drugs from longshoremen. I only sold for about a year.

With all the drinking and drugs, I started beating on my wife and the kids. I know that's a bad excuse, but I didn't feel like I had control of my life. I went to my first detox because I had started to become violent when I was drunk, so I knew I had to go. I wanted to quit. I went to detox in Vancouver for five days, then a treatment centre in Maple Ridge for seven weeks. The Longshoremen helped me pay for it. That time I was sober for three years.

When I was at Maple Ridge, my wife came to see me twice. My counsellor talked to her and then he told me that I better learn how to wash the dishes and do the laundry. That was his way of telling me that she wasn't coming back.

She did come back, but I relapsed, and we split up for good and she took the kids back with her to her reserve for her and their safety. We would try and get back together, but I was just too deep into my addiction. It was the same old thing. She had good reason for leaving. I felt so alone in the empty house after she left; there's nothing worse than an empty house. It hit me pretty hard. My answer to that was to drink more.

14

Drowning

WHEN I'D SOBERED UP, they'd given me a program: I had to go to meetings, talk to my Creator. I had to do everything, but I gradually stopped. I quit going to meetings. I quit talking to my Creator. I'd try to quit drinking, but I went back to it each time. I remember buying a bottle one time after I'd been sober for a while – it was Canadian Club – and pouring it into a glass in the kitchen. That glass sat there for a long time. I was alone, and I knew where it was going to go, but I said *Eff it* and the trip started all over again.

I wasn't even aware of the drinking being connected to residential school. The anger would surface, and the tears would too. It was the only time I'd cry. It would come up when I was drinking, but I didn't want to think about it. I didn't want to know why I was shaped the way I was. Thinking back now, with all the drinking and the drugs I was trying to mask the pain from residential school. It would work for a while, but then it would come back in a different form: anger.

Unfortunately, I wasn't a good father to my kids back in them days. I was too wrapped up in my own thing, wanting to party all the time and chase women. I do remember one thing I did as a dad back then, in part because it involved the same nuns I had dealt with at St. Paul's. Their order, called the Sisters of the Child Jesus, ran a school in North Van called St. Edmund's. My oldest son went to school there. I guess some other kid had told their parents that they saw one of the nuns hit him. He never told either me or his mother. When I got wind of it, after the other kid's mother called me, I was furious. I marched down to the school and pulled my son out of there that same day. When the nuns tried asking me why I was doing what I was doing, I had two words for them: "Fuck off."

Another time, not all that long after pulling my kids from that school, I was at a church bazaar that they used to have on the reserve. A lot of times, the nuns from St. Edmund's would be there. At one of these bazaars, I saw one of the real bad nuns from St. Paul's walking around. I was fuming mad on the inside, but I didn't want to make a big scene. Instead, I just stared her down. Wherever she walked, my eyes followed. I guess she finally felt the glare because she turned around and looked at me. When she made out who I was, she turned again, but this time to find an exit and leave. As long as I went to those bazaars, I never saw her again.

Like I said, I wasn't a good father when I was mixed up in all the craziness with the booze and drugs, but whenever I was sober, or was trying to get sober, I did my best. When I wasn't messed up, I would make an effort to see my kids every weekend. The boys and I always had a good time. I didn't really have any idea what I was supposed to be doing, so I would just let them lead the way. We'd go to the park or to the movies, whatever they wanted. They seemed to be enjoying themselves and that always made me happy.

For a long time, though, I would try to get sober and then fall right back into it, sink further and further into my addiction. It was a wild time. Sometimes I'd be at a party, drinking away, and someone would come over, tell me to open my mouth, and throw something in there. I didn't know what I was taking. Whether it was LSD, Quaaludes, or whatever, it didn't matter. As long as I was getting high.

I met my second wife through a mutual friend that I knew through the Alcoholics Anonymous program. At that time, she was having a real tough go and needed a hand. She was actually living with her kid in a garage that had been made into a makeshift suite off an alleyway in Vancouver. My friend was asking around to see if anyone had any extra plates or cutlery. I gave him a few things for her. When he said that he was going to buy her some groceries and drop them off, I tagged along. When I met her, we were attracted to one another right away. We started dating and she moved in not too long after. We got married really quickly. The trouble was that when we actually got to know one another, we really didn't care for each other. It was made all the more difficult by the fact that we adopted my cousin's baby – a little girl – right out of the hospital because my cousin was drinking at the time. So was I, but at least I had a house and a job. I also became pretty close with my wife's eight- or nine-year-old son. The problem was really that my new wife and I didn't understand one another's feelings and emotions. The drink and the drugs didn't help either. She would always complain about how unavailable and irresponsible I was.

"You're just like a kid, you know. I have to do everything for you! I got to cook for you, wash your clothes, get you up in the morning, tell you to go to work," she'd say. It was all true.

All of my wives did all those things. My life just kept getting worse. Our marriage lasted for only a few years before she left. Funnily enough, she was the first person to ever get the authorities involved when we were separating. I think it had something to do with her being white. It was a messy ordeal. She got me arrested a few times; not to say that I didn't deserve it – I was violent with her. I'd been sober during much of our relationship, but I'd always start drinking again eventually. When she left, she took both the kids with her, and I was alone again.

After I separated from my second wife, I just kept going deeper and deeper into my partying ways. I met my third wife at a party, a big drug party. We started talking, and two days later we were madly in love. She was Indigenous, from Vancouver Island, but her mother had married a Squamish man and she was quite into Squamish culture, doing things like going to the Longhouse. We did quite a bit of culture together. I didn't want to get married again, but she did, so we planned a wedding.

My third wife's cousins sold Native arts and crafts at the Capilano Mall, and she worked for them. For some reason, she wanted to get married at the mall, so we did. The mall set up an altar and everything. I felt weird, like we were on display. They even announced it over the mall's loudspeaker, saying something like, "Ladies and gentlemen, if you go down to the end of the mall, we're going to have a wedding!" People even showed up to see us, me in my rented tux and her in her white suit.

From the beginning of the marriage, I kept on being messed up with the drinking and drugs. By that time, my whole world revolved around my addiction. It was the eighties by now, and I was doing lots of cocaine on top of the drinking. Little did I know that my wife's love would soon come to be one of my biggest inspirations for getting clean.

One March, I went on a huge bender. That year, Easter fell in March; I know because I started partying on the Monday and wound up getting back home at seven o'clock in the morning on Good Friday. I was in really bad shape. I hadn't slept in days. I had stayed up drinking and doing coke. When I finally showed up back at home, I was really paranoid and suffering from psychosis. I had walked a really long way to get back home, and the whole time I was really angry. When I walked in the house, I made for the bedroom and opened up the door. My wife was lying in the bed. What happened next is hard to describe. When I saw her lying there, I was overcome with this feeling that I had to kill her. Following my insanity, I walked into the kitchen, opened up the cutlery drawer, and wrapped my hand around the biggest butcher knife that we had. For whatever reason, as I held on to that knife, a wave of goodness came over me, telling me to stop. I let go of the knife, closed the drawer, and walked outside. It was a really nice day out. I sat down on the steps in front of our house and started crying. My wife must have heard me because soon after she came and sat beside me outside.

"What are you doing out here?" she asked. I told her that I was going to kill her. She looked me in the eyes and said, "I would have forgiven you." In that moment, I was certain she did not understand what I had meant, that perhaps I was not being clear. I re-explained myself.

"I was going to kill you."

"I know," she said softly.

I broke down. "I don't want to be like this anymore. I need help," I said through my tears.

She told me to wait where I was, went inside, and made a phone call. Around half an hour later two drug and alcohol counsellors showed up. They asked me to come with them to a detox centre. I agreed. I was forty-six years old and thought my life was over.

15

Tsow-Tun Le Lum

WHEN I GOT TO the detox centre, I was in a really bad way.
As much as I wanted to quit, my addiction fought me tooth
and nail. I thought I was fooling everybody there because I
had a pocket, and a belly, full of Tylenol 3s. When I got to
the detox centre check-in, I was so stoned I could barely sit
upright, let alone write my name. I kept the charade up. The
next day, still high as kite, I saw all these detox patients
lining up for these pills from the nurse there. All these guys
would go up and open their mouth, the nurse would put the
pill in their mouth, and they would swallow it in front of her.
Fifteen minutes later, all of these guys who got the pill would
be sitting there all chilled out and relaxed. I went up to the
nurse and asked her what the pills were for. She told me that
they were to stop convulsions. *I got to get me some of those,*
I thought to myself. So the day after, still high as ever on the
Tylenol 3s, I got into the line with all the registered patients.
When I got to the nurse, with my name obviously not on the
list, I bullshitted my way into getting a dose.

I always say that that was the best worst thing I ever did.
Whatever those pills were, when they mixed with the T3s,
they gave me terrible hallucinations. That night when I went
to bed, I could see and feel all these little men pulling at my

blankets, hair, and nose. It was so uncomfortable. When I woke up the next morning, I walked over to the toilet and dumped the rest of the drugs I had on me. I would like to say that it was a beautiful moment, but it wasn't. Now that I had actually gone drug-free, I started detoxing.

Detoxing is a horrible experience. You can't get out of your bed, and you're sweating, all clammy. You can smell the coke coming out of you, all the drugs you did. And you have this nauseous feeling that grips your stomach and won't let go. The worst part of it all is that there is nothing anyone can do about it. Even things that usually feel good, like a shower, don't help you any. Your only choice is to ride it out.

After my detox was complete, the detox centre sent me on an eighteen-hour bus trip to a recovery house up in Creston. I ended up staying there for seven weeks. It was kind of like an extended detox. It was a place where people went to really dry out. At Creston, I experienced my first sweat. At first, I went to the Sweat Lodge just to watch. I'd stand at the window and watch others doing the sweat. The man who ran the sweats would cut the wood and make the fire and stack up the rocks, and he'd wave at me. When I got a bit braver, I'd go down with him and end up helping with the wood and the fire. I'd bring the rocks into the Sweat Lodge, and pretty soon I was in there.

Everyone warned me it would be really hot. Everyone told me not to be afraid to ask for the door, not to be afraid to lie down, but I loved it. I could really feel it. You pray to the Creator and you can feel that your prayers are being heard. The fire of the Sweat Lodge reminded me of the strength I had inside myself, and no matter what had happened to me, that strength was still there.

After my stay at Creston, I went to a rehabilitation centre called Tsow-Tun Le Lum, over in Lantzville on Vancouver Island. They also have a Sweat Lodge there and I went.

Tsow-Tun Le Lum ended up being a place of real healing for me. It was the place where I was forced to go inside and figure out what I was holding on to that made me act so destructively. They made me write down everything: why I drank, what was hurting me. They called me on everything. If I exaggerated or made excuses, they'd say, "Bullshit." At Tsow-Tun Le Lum, I wrote so much that by time I left, I had a thick pile of papers filled with everything that had happened to me.

By writing it down, I could make the connections between everything. I realized I was dysfunctional and I drank a lot to cover up the things that hurt. I hurt a lot from residential school, but it was better to drink than to cry, so I'd drink and then lose control and get violent. I blamed that on my drinking, but my counsellor told me that was an excuse. I had excuses for everything. I realized that I felt unloved at residential school, so I didn't love myself. It's pretty hard to care about anyone else when you don't love yourself. It's not conscious; it's just that you accept that this is the way it is. When I wrote it all down, I could see everything. It was hard to do, but once I did it, I began to feel better because it was outside of me.

There was another exercise we used to do at the treatment centre. All of us recovering addicts would sit in a circle with the counsellor and share. You could say as much or as little as you were willing to, but you had to share. Whenever it was your turn, the last guy would pass over an Eagle feather. For the first week and a half I was there, anytime anyone would try to pass me the Eagle feather, I would decline. Finally, after ten days of this, the counsellor called me into her office.

"Sam, do you want to go home?" she asked.

"No," I said defiantly. I thought I had been doing a good job.

She replied, "How come? You aren't taking part in any-thing. You just sit there. You don't say anything besides that you're doing good."

"Well, what do you want me to do?" I asked back.

"You have to talk about what's inside you. You have to tell me what's wrong with you," she explained.

"I don't know how to do that."

"I'll help you."

And she did. She helped me get out all the abuse and shame that I felt, all the stuff I had been holding on to for almost forty years. I opened up as much as I could. I told her things that I had never told anyone before. I told her that I had been sexually abused. I didn't really tell her any details about who or what; I wasn't ready. She was really considerate. She never pushed me; she was just there for me. That was big for me. Before that, I carried a lot of hurt and pain inside me. I was sexually assaulted, bullied by other kids, beat up, and slapped around, and I never told anyone – not even my wives or brothers – about being sexually molested. I was too ashamed, so I hid it all that time, and I was packing all that pain around with me. Even at the treat-ment centre, where lots of people had been to residential school, no one admitted to anyone else that they'd been sexually assaulted. At St. Paul's, I know there must have been other boys. There were others with beds near mine, and the nun would pick one of us. All of those other boys died young. Because of carrying all that around, before that inter-action with my counsellor, when somebody would ask me what was wrong, I would just say, "Nothing," but I'd say it in an angry way, so they knew it meant to back off. After I opened up and unpacked everything I was holding on to, I was finally free from my past. The wounds that I had suf-fered all those years ago in that residential school could now be healed.

Almost every one of us at the treatment centre had experienced the same trauma and abuse at those schools. I felt that I was in the right place, being at that treatment centre. It hurt to listen to everyone sharing their stories. Not because it happened to me, too, but because they were grown men, crying. If you passed those guys on the street, you would never know that they were victims of that violence. My older sister, Margaret, also went through the same treatment program as me.

Changing friends, going to regular meetings, and praying helped me the most throughout my healing journey. I used to go to two or three meetings a day. I used to get up at six thirty in the morning, catch a bus, make it to the treatment centre for a seven o'clock meeting, then go to a noon meeting, a three o'clock meeting, an eight o'clock meeting, and end my day with an eleven o'clock meeting. Going to those meetings was another way of handling my loneliness because I'd feel good after. I had a lot of baggage, hurt, and pain, and I'd get to leave it all at the door; after an hour, though, I'd walk outside and pick up that baggage again. That went on until I really looked at myself and said, *Yeah, this is what I've got to do*.

A few years after I got clean, my wife and I separated. She packed a bag and told me she was going to the Island for a while, but from the size of her bag, I knew she was leaving. We were together for thirteen years. She was a good woman. In truth, once I was sober the writing was on the wall.

After treatment, I became much more reliable at work. Before that, I'd sometimes only make two hundred dollars a week when I could have made a thousand. There were lots of guys who didn't want to work with me then. When I stopped drinking, I found out there were guys at work who didn't drink. I had to find new people to hang out with.

I met my fourth wife in 2007, through her son, who was going through the same addiction treatment program that I had gone through. He brought her to a meeting after his one-year cake, a celebration of his being clean for a year, and we started talking. Eventually we started seeing each other. Maybe three or four months later, we moved in together, and we got married after I got a settlement from the government. We had quite a big wedding, and it was ceremonial: there was a Sweat Lodge and a Sundance. Even the band was from Alcoholics Anonymous. Delana, a blues singer, also played at our wedding. I remember it was the hottest day of the year. I had to go out and rent fans for everybody. Our cake was melting because it was so hot. Overall, our relationship was pretty good, but eventually we divorced too.

I met Michelle through a friendship centre in 2016. Every time I saw her there, I would say hi and she would give me a big smile back. Eventually I asked her out on a date. She seemed pretty surprised when this old man showed up on a Harley to pick her up. Going to residential school makes it hard to have good relationships, but Michelle and I are happy together.

16

I'm Still Here

AROUND 2008, THE TRUTH about the Indian residential school system started surfacing. People started coming forward as Survivors. When I heard other people talk about the whole ordeal, I came forward as a Survivor myself. The first time I really spoke about the sexual abuse in detail was when I went to talk to my lawyer about getting the residential school settlement, before I went before the Indian residential school adjudicator (for the Independent Assessment Process). My lawyer – he was a white guy – told me that everyone he talked to got beat up, slapped around. Everyone got the strap, everyone was made to kneel down. It was a common story that someone had lost their hearing from being hit. He told me that and then he asked me if I'd been sexually abused. I was quiet as I thought about it, and he said, "You were, weren't you?"

That lawyer was the first person I told all the details to. It was hard. I remember after I told him, I left his office, I sat down on a bench in a park, and I cried. I had to tell him everything so that he could write it up for the Independent Assessment Process. The process actually took place at a hotel that they used as a kind of court. I had support with me: I had my lawyer, my fourth wife, and a counsellor when

I went to tell my story. Sometimes I had to take a break. My lawyer had recorded and printed everything I'd told him and had already given it to the adjudicator, who asked me questions about it all. Tell me about the abuse. Tell me about the sexual assault. Who did it? What happened? How often? This was the first time I'd spoken publicly about the sexual abuse. It hurt to bring it all out again and to relive it.

With the adjudicator and the lawyers, it was all about money, you know, because you're not going to get anything else back.

I went to the Sweat Lodge before I went to their court and again after. That helped a lot. My culture saved me.

When I first adopted the sweats, it helped to talk to a Creator who wasn't going to punish me. There was no hell or purgatory. It felt good just to know the Ancestors were listening to my prayers. Just to know they were there. When I got initiated into the Longhouse, I called the ones who initiated me Dad, and the ones who helped them I called them Mom. I drummed and I sang and then I became a Sundancer. Eventually, I began to initiate others. When I started to initiate others, they called me Dad. That means I worked on them. It's meaningful. I've come back to my culture and helped others – younger people – come into it. Sweats. Sundance. These things saved me. I've been doing them for more than twenty years. Now I'm a Sundance Chief.

Connecting with my culture helped me recover from addiction and also from residential school. It helps you get the bad feelings out.

Now there are younger Squamish people practising more and more culture, even learning the language. My granddaughter speaks the Squamish language fluently. She even teaches it; it's her full-time job. One of my grandsons can also speak it. It used to be that you'd only hear the old-timers talking to each other in the language, but now the only time I hear it is when young kids get together and they're talking away. When the younger generation gets together, they greet each other by saying "sẹkw'í7tel."[1] My granddaughter says it means family or relatives. The language has changed. The younger people don't use the same guttural sounds; it's evolving for the younger generation. I never dreamed – after everything – that would happen.

Another way I connect with my culture is through hunting. I learned to hunt on my own. I was always a good shot. My dad told me that you always shoot to get the heart, or if you're a good shot, you go for the eye or the neck. I never thought I was good enough to get the eye or the neck, so I'd go for the heart.

Hunting connects me to my culture because we eat a lot of deer meat. I first went out with some Elders and they taught me how to dress an animal. They were my guides. Another time, I went up with one of my son's good friends and he knew a guy from Prince George who really knew hunting. They lived it. We went out and we got a moose and the guy from Prince George showed me how to gut a moose. He asked, "Do you know how to clean a fish?" I do, so he told me just to think of it as a fish. You cut a little hole in the neck and then you cut from there and pull everything out.

Now I sometimes hunt with my grandson. He likes hunting; he's got a rifle and everything. When we hunt, we say a prayer before we get there and I promise the Grandmothers and the Grandfathers a plate if they help me get an animal, so every time I get one, I make a fire and put out a plate for them and offer it up to them. One time I said I'd offer them a plate and I didn't do it, and then my freezer broke down and all the meat spoiled. That was the Ancestors telling me I

....

1   Pronounced *[see-quad-ell]*.

didn't come through. They were teaching me a lesson. Making an offering like that is our way.

After I got sober, I became a drug and alcohol counsellor with the Longshoremen Local 500. Another guy who became sober asked if I'd help him help other guys. A lot of times my boss would say, "So-and-so's drinking too much. Either he goes to treatment or he gets de-registered." My boss would tell me to go and talk to the guy, so I'd go knock on his door and say "Local 500 sent me to talk to you." We'd sit down and I'd give him the options and tell the guy he could talk to me. And then I'd drive him out to the treatment centre and communicate with him while he was in there. We'd even go to meetings together.

After retiring as a longshoreman in 2008, I have continued to work as a drug and alcohol counsellor. Who better to counsel than a guy with so much experience? Up until COVID-19, I visited and supported men at the same treatment centre that I got clean at, on the Island. It feels good to be able to look them in the eye and tell them that I have been right where they are, tell them that I know what they're going through. Usually that will help them to open up, and that means a great deal to me.

I've been going to Tsow-Tun Le Lum as an Elder for a long time – since 1991, actually. I was a very young Elder at first. Eventually, they started taking prisoners into the program there. Some of them were just there to get away from prison – you could tell – but some of them really wanted to change. Before COVID-19, I'd go there maybe once every three months. I'd rotate with the other Elders and stay for a week at a time. It used to be for two weeks, but they cut it down.

In the morning I'd attend meetings, and then again in the afternoon. Everyone speaks, and then I'd speak. I'd tell them everything I did and how I finally got sober. I have the experience to talk to those guys. It makes me feel good to help them. Sometimes I'd see those guys later on and they'd thank me. Most of the guys there are Indigenous, so I felt like I could guide them on their journey. Nowadays a lot of the men are children of residential school Survivors. It used to be mostly residential school Survivors, but now I can see the trauma that's passed down. I'm lucky that I could break it. You have to change.

My experience as a Survivor today is much different from when I first started my healing journey. St. Paul's stole my childhood and a lot of my culture. In the past, I didn't look at myself as a Survivor. I simply thought of my experiences as some garbage that had happened in my life. Today I accept that St. Paul's happened, I acknowledge it, I talk about it, and I no longer live in the past. In the past, when I used to talk about residential school, the pain would come, and today it's not there. I mean, it is a little bit, but it doesn't consume me like before. The trauma caused me to turn to drinking and drugging, which is why I stayed away from my culture. Once I got sober and adopted the sweats and Sundance and began to practise my culture, I began to feel closer to the Creator. I have always felt a connection to the Creator, like he was listening to me most of the time, and he was helping me. I also believe that when I go into ceremony, I talk to my Grandfathers and Grandmothers, and I feel that they're present because they prayed for me a lot. Life looked pretty good once I got my sobriety back.

I don't think too much about the Truth and Reconciliation Commission (TRC) or the reparations program because, in my opinion, reconciliation wasn't really there; reconciliation is still not really there. It's a lot of government words, but they've done nothing, and everything that they want done is put on Indigenous Peoples' shoulders. I didn't get too involved with the TRC because I think it's all bullshit. Even when [former Prime Minister Stephen] Harper read that letter, he just had a piece of paper that somebody else wrote. You could tell there were no emotions, no feelings, when he read off that paper. In all honesty, when our reserve recreational centre played that 2008 speech on a big screen, I got up and walked out.

For reconciliation to happen, I think Canadians should know that the Indian residential school system happened. They should know what happened there and how it affected us. A few years ago, a writer from *The Province* was writing very derogatory stories about Natives. When I read them, I kept on getting angrier and angrier. I picked up my phone and I called *The Province* to speak with her directly. She got on the phone, we had a conversation, and then we met for lunch. It turned out that St. Paul's was located on the same road she lived on, and she didn't know that it was a residential school. She didn't have a clue about what went on. I explained to her that most of the people she was writing about were in pain, and that even we couldn't understand why we were the way we were. After I told her the truth about what happened at those schools, she never wrote a thing about Indigenous people again.

I don't know what reconciliation means to me. The violence and trauma have been going on for so long. For my whole life. There's us and them, and by "them" I mostly mean the government. For example, the Indian Act, which we are ruled by, was written in 1876, and there have barely been any changes made to it. To this day, the government still uses it and I think it's still about control. According to them, we are the problem, and we are the problem because we own the land. It all comes down to ownership of the land. And I know how long we've been on this land. Once I was at a beach in our territory and I just had a feeling that I should dig around; I found a bone needle. Our people were there.

One time, I was asked to sit on a committee to speak with four representatives of the government about what they could do to make us happy or make life better for us. They were all white. I really went into them and changed the whole atmosphere of the meeting. I called them out for always talking about doing this and that for us but reminded them that they never actually did anything. I told them that they should let us care for ourselves. I reminded them that Indigenous Peoples have been here for tens of thousands of years, and we're still here. I told them that one day they will be gone, but our people will still be here. After I gave it to them, I left that meeting. The other Natives in attendance told me that I changed the whole meeting because I was the only one who spoke up. Ultimately, I was just tired of white people coming in to decide what will make us happy. All we want is for them to let us live our lives and to not be dependent on them. That's why I became a longshoreman. I decided I was not going to depend on the settler government.

My hope for future generations is for independence. I want the future generations to not be dependent on the settler government. I want them to work and be happy with what they're doing, or be happy with wherever their lives might lead them. I want the future generations to live their own lives and have the freedom to be themselves. When I think about the future generations, I think about my granddaughter, my baby. She lived with me for seven years, and I gave her the freedom she deserves. Today she is thirteen years old and very outspoken, but I am still her Papa. My fourth wife took her with her when we separated, but my granddaughter still phones me about twice a month. We always enjoyed our snuggle time, and I loved that. I also always allow her to express herself and encourage her to be who she wants to be. When she was a baby, I called her One Sock because she always seemed to have only one sock on. But she could dance! Once, when she was only about eighteen months old, she danced at a Sundance. She had that spirit in her. Recently, she had bullies picking on her and she reported it. I'm glad she did. I am happy she was able to stand up for herself because I couldn't when I was a child in residential school.

In the summer of 2021, after the news about the unmarked graves at Kamloops Residential School came out, I visited the school with my two sons. They almost sent me to that school, but it was full up. It was touching to go. You could feel it. I could feel it, that there was someone looking out the windows, looking at me. Kids. Because I'm an Elder, they let me visit the graves. I talked to them and told them who I am, that my name is Sam, and I'm Squamish, I'm an Elder, and I know what they went through. At Kamloops, I offered the children prayers.

Now there's talk of using ground-penetrating radar at St. Paul's. A lot of the grounds have been paved over (to make way for St. Thomas Aquinas School), but I went up there and I seen where we dug that hole. It's still there. It hasn't been paved over.

Since Kamloops, I went to visit Charlie's grave. I was surprised to see that it has a proper grave marker. It has his name on it – Charlie Lucas. It felt good to see it. Now I know where to find him.

With things like Kamloops coming out into the open, they're finally starting to teach what happened in the schools. They're getting honest, and I want everyone to know what really happened. I want everyone to know what it was like, what they did. That it was part of a genocide. They wanted us to not be Indians. They wanted to take that from us, and they succeeded. When I came out of there, I didn't like being Indian. I was ashamed of who I was. I was lost.

Today I am most proud of who I am. I'm proud to be a Native. I am no longer ashamed of it. I am proud that I changed. I was a criminal, I was in jail, and I changed all of that. I'm proud to think about how far I have come. Sometimes when anger pops up because of my experiences, I fight with myself to keep the anger down. I can still go to those dark places in my mind, and it's scary, but I'm proud that I can recognize it and control it. I am proud of the way I think today. I can take care of myself, when I couldn't do that in the past because I had been institutionalized. I endured residential school, spent four and half years in prison, and even my marriages took care of me, but today I can do it myself. I learned how to survive.

AFTERWORD

On Co-writing Sam George's Memoir

EVERYTHING BEGINS WITH a story, which, as the writer Thomas King says, is "all we are." The stories we are taught and the stories we tell have the power to shape our world views, our identities, ourselves.

My name is Jill Yechiela Yonit Goldberg. It's a mouthful that reveals the story of where I come from and what ancestry I can claim as mine. *Goldberg* is the last name my paternal grandfather chose to call himself when he came to this country from Eastern Europe. *Yonit* is the Hebrew word for dove or small dove; my parents were inspired by a war in a faraway country to give me this name. *Yechiela* is for my maternal grandfather, Yechiel, who, like all of my grandparents, came to Canada seeking freedom from the religious persecution that culminated in the Holocaust. My name marks me as a settler and a forever-guest on the unceded, ancestral, and contemporary territories of the xʷməθkʷəy̓əm (Musqueam), Sḵwx̱wú7mesh (Squamish), and Səl̓ílwətaʔ (Tsleil-Waututh) Peoples where I now live. I am the granddaughter of people who were spared from genocide and found peace and relative ease in Canada, all while this country was attempting its own form of genocide through Indian residential schools.

I did not grow up knowing this truth.

The nature of colonial injury includes, but is not limited to, erasure, and the education I received is an example of that. My schooling at all levels, including post-secondary, left out any information about residential schools, the history of colonization, and Indigenous cultures and languages. If stories are a way to share knowledge and pass on values, what values are taught when the stories of entire cultures are omitted from the curriculum? How can a settler learn respect and compassion, or realize the impact of their very presence in a given place, if they never learn the stories or the language of that place?

It can be hard to understand and to admit that in an educational context, what we teach, as much as what we do not teach, is a tacit way of expressing whose stories have value and what history is significant. The exclusion of Indigenous stories from my education could only have the effect of devaluing the Indigenous experience and dehumanizing Indigenous people. Erasure is a powerful form of discrimination that prevents learners not only from understanding the experiences of others but also from fully knowing their own place and role in history and society.

Fortunately, teaching, as I do at Langara College, has given me the opportunity to fill in the blind spots. In the years after the Truth and Reconciliation Commission of Canada was launched, I became aware of how much I did not know, and so I turned to the books and began to read and to learn. By 2017, I was teaching exclusively Indigenous writers in my first-year literature and composition classes and, in the years following, I began to teach an upper-level course on Indigenous literature.

Teaching these courses necessitated a reconsideration of the way in which I teach. After all, how could I teach what I didn't intimately know? Several collaborations were born of my desire to make sure my students read Indigenous literature. I worked with Rick Ouellet, former director of Indigenous Education and Services at Langara College, and with Langara's Elder-in-residence and other Indigenous community members to select the material I taught, and I included these individuals as frequent guests in my classes, centring their experiences and their knowledge. In many ways, I began to view teaching as an opportunity to create a network based on co-operation and collaboration rather than an opportunity to enact a hierarchy that places the knowledge of the instructor above that of everyone else. By practising a community-oriented style of pedagogy, I was able to see myself as a co-learner and a guide more than an authority as I began to have an increasingly pluralistic experience of literature. Thus, the shift to more inclusive content created a shift to a more inclusive style of teaching. All this meant that when the opportunity arose to turn my Indigenous literature class into something bigger, the infrastructure was already in place.

My colleague Rachel Mines had been teaching a class called Writing Lives: The Holocaust Survivor Memoir Project, in which her students studied literature from the holocaust and then met with holocaust survivors, interviewing them and ultimately writing their memoirs. When Rachel was near retirement, she offered the course to me with the idea of transforming it so that students would study literature by Indigenous writers and then meet with and interview Elders who had attended residential schools, collaborating with them to write their memoirs as a way to add to the growing body of knowledge that sheds light on the darkness of the residential school system.

In 2019–20, teaching this course for the first time, I was able to partner with the Indian Residential School Survivors Society (IRSSS), which recruits the Elders who participate in the project. I have also continued to collaborate with other local Elders and with Indigenous Education and Services at Langara College.

For students, the Writing Lives course is not only about studying literature and learning how to conduct an interview. Students have the chance to practise important protocols for interacting with Elders, they are asked to put the needs of the Elders first, and they must collaborate with each other and with the Elders when it comes to the writing process. As anyone who teaches literature will tell you, language is not neutral: moving from orality to the written word requires careful attention to individual and cultural language patterns. By listening to Elders, and in being asked to edit their memoirs in a style that best represents their voices, meaning, and intentions, students come to understand that language itself, when handled with care, can be a tool for reconciliation. In the process of transcribing, writing, and editing, students (and I) are aided by Gregory Younging's foundational book *Elements of Indigenous Style: A Guide for Writing by and about Indigenous Peoples.* Once the draft memoirs are presented to the Elders, students go through a lengthy process of receiving approval for their work, teaching them about consultation, consent, and the meaning of self-determination for the Elders. In this way, Writing Lives enacts the values of listening to and centring the experiences, desires, and knowledge of Elders, thereby giving students the opportunity to participate in the type of learning and writing that has the potential to address the erasure and devaluation that is implicit in the colonial injury. For the Elders, it is an opportunity to have their stories heard, read, and included as the centrepiece of post-secondary pedagogy.

Readers, especially other instructors, may be interested to know more about the process through which the memoirs are created. During the first semester of Writing Lives, students work together to create an interview guide based on their studies of Indian residential schools and on information gleaned from guest speakers (Elders, a counsellor from the IRSSS, and a journalism instructor). Before meeting with Elders, students are required to complete the Government of Canada Panel on Research Ethics module on Ethical Conduct for Research, and they are also briefed by the IRSSS on protocols for interacting with Elders.

Before they meet, Elders and students are informed of their rights and obligations, and everyone involved signs contracts stipulating that the intellectual material resulting from the work of Writing Lives is the exclusive property of the Elder, and that only the Elder has the ability to make decisions concerning the use of the memoir and to profit from it in any way.

During the interview process, students record the Elders as they speak. The interviews are transcribed verbatim by the students, who then do the work of turning the transcript into a memoir. In some cases, information may be restructured or lightly edited for clarity; however, in the process of turning the transcripts into memoirs, nothing is altered, added, or omitted without consultation with and permission from the Elder. Once students complete a first draft of the memoirs, they give them to me for light editing of such things as punctuation and formatting. I then turn the memoir over to each Elder so that they can review it and ask for any changes they wish. The process is then repeated: the students make changes to the memoirs, I review them, and the Elders have the opportunity to ask for additional changes or to give their final approval to the work. In all cases, the Elders' wishes are strictly observed. Great care is taken to preserve their voice as well as their experience of autonomy over the stories as they were written down.

Finally, the memoirs are printed in multiples so that each Elder can give copies of their work to family members.

Students each receive one copy of the memoir they worked on; however, they are asked not to share it with anyone else without permission from the Elder. They are also asked to destroy the recordings, as per the contracts, and delete from their computers any material pertaining to the work they have done with the Elders and to maintain a degree of confidentiality suitable to the sensitivity of the stories that were shared.

Three students worked with Sam George: Liam Belson, Dylan MacPhee, and Tanis Wilson. The three students self-identify as settlers on Sk̲wx̲wú7mesh, xʷməθkʷəy̓əm, and Səl̓ílwəta association territories, with Wilson also identifying as Omaškêko (Swampy Cree) from northern Ontario. All three have been greatly influenced in their work, their activism, and their studies by their participation in the creation of this memoir.

After the first round of Writing Lives in 2020, Sam approached me and asked about getting his memoir published. We agreed to work together on this project, and it has been an honour and a very deep learning experience to work with him on submitting, writing, and editing this manuscript for publication. As we have worked together, I have followed the same process as the students: I have interviewed Sam, transcribed those interviews, and added additional material to the memoir. At every point in the process of querying, submitting, writing, and publication, Sam has reviewed the written material, and his wishes with respect to the content of this work have always been respected.

Teaching Writing Lives and subsequently working with Sam has been a gift for many reasons. It has increased my understanding of the ongoing and damaging effects of colonization and residential schools. Perhaps more significantly, it has put me in the fortunate position of witnessing the creation of a community that includes students, Elders, and others, as they learn to care for each other through the exchange of knowledge. It is my hope that this speaks to the demand for reconciliation in Canada.

Having gotten to know the stories of the Elders who have participated in Writing Lives with some intimacy, I can see that reconciliation is a very different project for settlers than it is for Indigenous people. As a xʷməθkʷəy̓əm Elder has said to me, every day requires dozens of acts of reconciliation on the part of Indigenous individuals: they must daily reconcile themselves to living on their own land while being or having been dispossessed of language, culture, heritage, and more. I believe that for settlers, reconciliation asks us to integrate knowledge of the harms of colonization into our contemporary understanding of our society and our place in it, to understand how we benefit from these harms, and to be accountable to this knowledge by teaching it to others, building relationships with Indigenous people/communities based on respect and reciprocity, and speaking up and standing up as allies and friends to Indigenous people by believing their stories and centring their needs in our learning and activism. Reconciliation is not only something someone else – the government or other institutions – needs to enact through policy. It is something settlers can enact in our relationships with each other, with Indigenous communities, and with the land.

In post-secondary circles, there's a lot of talk about Indigenization and decolonization as part of the project of reconciliation. Teaching Writing Lives has given me the opportunity to consider the meaning of each of these. I see Indigenization as the process of students learning about Indigenous culture and history and of learning to see the world through an Indigenous world view and social/cultural/historical frame. I see decolonization as the process of displacing power, shifting from a hierarchical to a collaborative mode by which who has knowledge, and what knowledge is valued, is altered.

As a non-Indigenous person and a settler, I have not always been comfortable talking about Indigenizing my course because I'm not certain it's my place to offer up Indigenous knowledge; however, by decentring myself and my experiences and creating the community necessary for Writing Lives to take place, I feel that the course is in many ways a functioning model of decolonization, which in turn allows Indigenization to happen. By making room for the Elders' and other community members' stories and putting them at the centre of our experience together, new knowledge can take shape, and this, I believe, is the task of education in the era of reconciliation.

Of a given story, Thomas King says, "It's yours. Do with it what you will ... But don't say in the years to come that you would have lived your life differently if only you had heard this story. You've heard it now."[1]

My name is Jill Yechiela Yonit Goldberg. Until I was an adult, I did not know the stories that come from this place, from the lands and the seas that have nurtured me all of my life. I was not taught any local language, and I did not know the pre-colonial names of the places I grew up loving. Writing Lives and working with Sam has altered all of that.

My reconciliation is in learning the ways in which my story is not one that emerges from the land I now occupy, in hearing the stories that do come from this place, and then in

....

1 Thomas King, "'You'll Never Believe What Happened' Is Always a Great Way to Start," in Read, Listen, Tell: Indigenous Stories from Turtle Island, eds. Sophie McCall, Deanna Reder, David Gaertner, and Gabrielle L'Hirondelle Hill (Waterloo: Wilfred Laurier Press, 2017), 62–77.

learning new ways of being present on this land. By learning Sam's story and participating in writing it down, I feel that in some way, I now carry the obligation to hold it with care, to share it, and to offer it to others who can learn from it.

A story, once told, will ripple outward into the world and change it, and that is why instructors can no longer choose to erase stories like Sam's. Reconciliation, if it is to come, demands change, and stories like Sam's are perhaps our best hope for the type of learning that ignites the fire of change.

– JILL YONIT GOLDBERG

READER'S GUIDE

THIS READER'S GUIDE is provided to assist students and instructors as they consider the cultural, social, psychological, historical, and political aspects of Elder Sam George's story. Though his is only one story, it reveals experiences with culture, colonization, and institutionalization that are common to many Survivors – both first-hand and intergenerational/community – of the Indian residential school system.

For readers who are settlers, this memoir offers an opportunity to better understand colonization, the Indian residential school system, and the pervasive impacts these things continue to have on Indigenous people and communities, and on the institutions (including schools) that govern and shape our society and therefore ourselves.

For students of disciplines such as social work, counselling, education, nursing, medicine, and law, among others, this book may provide background information that will help them become aware of ongoing societal inequities and injustices that emerged from colonization and the Indian residential school system, and to grapple with their role in creating communities that are safer, more equitable, and more just.

The goal of the Writing Lives course, from which the published version of this memoir emerged, is not only to have students learn about what happened in residential schools but also to build caring and trusting relationships with Survivors that allow the students to implicate themselves in the sharing of their stories, thereby becoming accountable to these stories in the rest of their lives. Readers of Sam George's story are invited to consider the same: by knowing Sam's story, how can you be accountable to it?

The reader's guide begins with some background information on residential schools and the history of colonization. It then asks questions specific to the memoir and concludes by looking at the legacy of residential schools and exploring actions that individuals can take to contribute to the work of reconciliation.

RESIDENTIAL SCHOOLS

Residential schools were set up and funded by the Canadian government and administered by churches. The schools first opened in the 1880s; the last one closed in 1996. Although the schools provided some perfunctory "education," their real goal was the cultural assimilation of Indigenous children who, it was hoped, would go on to lose their ties to their culture, ancestry, and territories. Children were forcibly removed from their family homes. Speaking their native languages and practising their culture was forbidden in the schools. It was common for children to be beaten and otherwise severely punished; sexual abuse was rampant. The conditions in the schools were poor, with disease and malnourishment endemic. Many of the schools emphasized prayer and manual labour over academic learning.

Rooted in the same historical attitudes that shaped colonization, residential schools can be understood as an extension of colonization's project of dominating and exploiting land and resources and subjugating Indigenous Peoples.

Canada's first prime minister, Sir John A. Macdonald, commissioned journalist and politician Nicholas Flood Davin to study the American system of industrial schools for Indigenous children. In his 1879 "Report on Industrial Schools for Indians and Half-Breeds," Davin recommended that Canada copy the United States' attempts to aggressively assimilate Indigenous children by taking them from their parents and communities and "civilizing" them through a process of "education."

Reflecting on Canada's political aim of assimilation and its desire to seize land from Indigenous Peoples, what do you understand to be the goals of residential schools?

In his report, Davin wrote, "If anything is to be done with the Indian, we must catch him very young. The children must be kept constantly within the circle of civilized conditions."

What assumptions about Indigenous culture versus European culture are implicit in this remark?

As the attitudes and ideas that shaped residential school were similar to those that shaped colonization, it's useful to know about earlier documents, including the Doctrine of Discovery, which was the basis for colonization, and the Indian Act, which was and still is the legal document that outlines the relationship between Canada and Indigenous Peoples.

The Doctrine of Discovery

The Papal Bull "Inter Caetera," issued by Pope Alexander VI on May 4, 1493, was a document that gave Spanish so-called explorers the "right" to claim lands that were "discovered" in the "New World" (e.g., the Americas). More broadly, the Bull stated that any land not inhabited by Christians was available to be acquired and exploited by Christian rulers, declaring that, "the Catholic faith and the Christian religion be exalted and be everywhere increased and spread, that the health of souls be cared for and that barbarous nations be overthrown and brought to the faith itself." This doctrine, known today as the Doctrine of Discovery, became the foundation of all European claims of territory in the Americas, and its attitude of domination and "ownership" of land and subjugation of non-Christian Peoples became the basis for interactions between settlers and Indigenous Peoples and, subsequently, for the Indian Act in Canada.

How do you think the Doctrine of Discovery and the attitudes inherent in it influenced the creation of residential schools and the way in which those who ran the schools treated Indigenous children?

The Indian Act

The Indian Act of 1876 is a federal document that lays out the handling of so-called Indian status, First Nations governance, and the management of reserve lands. Its origins can be traced back to the Gradual Civilization Act of 1857, which was an attempt to forcibly assimilate "Treaty Indians" (those who were registered as being a member of a band that had signed a treaty with the Crown and therefore had certain treaty rights) into Canadian settler society.

In 1920, Duncan Campbell Scott, then deputy superintendent of what was then called the Department of Indian Affairs, pushed for and saw passed an amendment to the Indian Act that made residential school attendance mandatory for all Indigenous children under fifteen years of age. Scott stated:

I want to get rid of the Indian problem. I do not think as
a matter of fact, that the country ought to continuously
protect a class of people who are able to stand alone ...
Our objective is to continue until there is not a single
Indian in Canada that has not been absorbed into the
body politic and there is no Indian question, and no
Indian Department, that is the whole object of this Bill.
(https://www.facinghistory.org/en-ca/resource-library/
until-there-not-single-indian-canada)

Consider the relationship between the legal policy of assimilation and the creation of residential schools.

*Does learning about the Indian Act and its policies of forcible
assimilation change your perspective on the intentions of those who
created the schools? If so, how?*

In 1904, a man named Peter Henderson Bryce, a medical
doctor, was appointed chief medical health officer for the
federal Department of Indian Affairs. In response to information suggesting that many children were dying at the residential schools, Bryce was tasked by the federal government
with investigating the schools and writing a report. His
report, submitted in 1907, was very critical of the conditions
in residential schools, which he noted were responsible for
the very high death rate (between 14 percent and 24 percent)
among Indigenous students.

Bryce's recommendations were dismissed, however, and
his access to research funds was discontinued. In response,
he wrote a pamphlet in 1922 called *The Story of a National
Crime: An Appeal for Justice to the Indians of Canada,* outlining
how the government was responsible for the terrible conditions at residential schools and how it had absolved itself of

responsibility for those conditions, which had resulted in so many deaths.

Why do you think the federal government suppressed the information Dr. Bryce wished to share, instead of focusing on improving the conditions of the schools?

Chief Shingwauk's Vision

In 1832, Shingwauk, a well-respected Anishinaabe Chief, snowshoed from Sault Ste. Marie to York in order to advocate before Governor John Colborne for education for his people. His vision was of a "Teaching Wigwam Lodge" where Indigenous people would not only learn to read and write English in order to adapt to the presence of European settlers, but would also learn their traditions and culture. Chief Shingwauk's vision was not realized at the time, but it did lead to the creation of the post-secondary institute Shingwauk Kinoomaage Gamig in 2008.

How do you think the realization of Chief Shingwauk's vision in place of residential schools would have altered the course of history?

THE FIRE STILL BURNS

The following pages explore questions specific to *The Fire Still Burns* while asking you to consider this story within the larger context of the legacy of colonization and the Indian residential school system.

Before reading this memoir, what did you know about residential schools?

How would you have described residential schools compared with what you have now read?

Land, Ancestry, and Identity

In the very first paragraph, Sam George situates himself within his family lineage and within a specific place.

From the way in which Sam situates himself, what is your understanding of the importance of ancestry and its connection with the land in Indigenous and Squamish culture?

What episodes from the first and second chapters illustrate this connection? Discuss their significance to the formation of young Sam's sense of self.

Sam identifies himself as being from Eslhá7an. As he notes, the colonized name for it is the Mission Reserve.

Do you think settlers would relate to places differently if we/they knew local Indigenous place names and their meanings and stories? If yes, how?

On page 5, Sam introduces his Ta'ah, who tells Sam, "Your name is Tseatsultux." Sam tells us this is a name that goes back five generations in his family.

Why do you think the nuns call Sam "number 3" instead of either his traditional name or even just Sam?

From what you've read, discuss the importance of Ta'ah in Sam's life.

Consider, also, what it meant that he was separated from her and her knowledge during the time he attended St. Paul's Indian Residential School.

How does the rupture in this relationship inform your understanding of intergenerational trauma and loss?

On page 7, Sam describes the older generation speaking to each other in the Squamish language. In the final chapter, Sam describes his granddaughter also speaking Squamish.

What do you think is lost when language is lost?

What do you think is the importance of the resurgence of Indigenous languages?

How would you describe the setting and atmosphere of the earliest years of Sam's life?

What seem to be the guiding values of these years?

Life at School

Starting on page 27, Sam describes his first moments at St. Paul's, when he is stripped, is covered in pesticide, and has his head shaved.

What do you think is the meaning of each of these violations? Why would the nuns have imposed such a brutal entry into St. Paul's?

Early on in his stay at St. Paul's, Sam notes the division between girls and boys, who were not permitted to interact.

What does this tell you about the values of the school, or the church running the school, as compared with the values in Sam's family?

On page 31, Sam notes that the nuns and priests ate good food while the students at St. Paul's were chronically undernourished. Later, on page 32, he writes that the older boys always tried to look after the younger ones by feeding them when they could.

What does this reveal about the nuns' and the priests' feelings about the children?

What do you learn about the values and culture among Sam and his peers?

On page 33, Sam describes the Musqueam boys who were speaking their language (hənq̓əmin̓əm̓)[1] in class and were beaten as a result. He also notes that although the students at St. Paul's had to recite Mass in Latin, no one ever taught them the meaning of the words.

If students come to associate their language with beatings, what do you imagine this does to their cultural identity and sense of self?

What do you think the fact that they were never taught the meaning of the words says about the way in which religion was taught at residential school?

Sam also describes the students at St. Paul's sometimes resisting their abusers.

Find instances of resistance and discuss. What do you think is the value of resistance, even if it results in punishment?

The Effects of Residential Schools
In 2001, Dr. Charles Brasfield identified a constellation of symptoms similar to those of post-traumatic stress disorder that he calls residential school syndrome. One of the symptoms, according to Brasfield, is "diminished interest and participation in aboriginal cultural activities and markedly deficient knowledge of traditional culture and skills."

....

1   *Pronounced [HUN-kuh-MEE-num].*

For many Survivors of the Indian residential school system, a return to their culture is healing. But if they have been taught to reject their own culture, how might this inhibit or delay healing?

Even though Sam's parents both attended St. Paul's, he notes that he didn't know much about the school before he went (p. 23) and explains that being a second-generation residential school Survivor meant that he didn't grow up with much affection (p. 21). He also says that the children going away to residential school fuelled the use of alcohol on the part of the parents (p. 22).

In addition to the abuse suffered by residential school students, how do you understand the impact residential school would have had on students who went on to become parents?

Why do you think Sam's parents didn't discuss residential school much?

Does it surprise you that the intergenerational effects of residential school travel not only from parent to child, but also from child to parent? Discuss how this is so and what it might mean for affected families.

The story of Charlie's death at St. Paul's is certainly one of the most traumatizing things Sam recalls about his time at the school.

Consider all the people who would have been affected by the loss of Charlie: his parents, who might never have known what happened to him; his sister, who was also at the school; all of his extended family; and his peers at the school. When you multiply this by the other estimated four thousand to six thousand children who are believed to have died at the schools,[2] what do you imagine is the total impact of losses like this one on Indigenous communities?

On page 55, Sam notes that he didn't talk about the sexual abuse he endured at St. Paul's until many years later.

Why do you think Sam kept silent for so long?

Do you think keeping silent makes healing more difficult?

On page 63, Sam says that, after coming home from St. Paul's, he no longer felt connected with his Ta'ah the way he had previously.

Why do you think it would be difficult for Sam resume a relationship with his Ta'ah?

Sam loved and looked up to his older brother Andy, but he gravely injured him in the fight that caused Sam to be sent to Oakalla. Sam turned to alcohol and drugs to deal with the pain he felt, but he explains that the alcohol, especially, made him feel anger, and he eventually began to take it out on his wives and kids.

What you to think caused Sam to have so much potential for violence in him?

While acknowledging that there's never an excuse for violence, what do you understand from this about the role of residential schools in contributing to addiction as well as to domestic and lateral violence?

....

2 *These are the numbers estimated by the Truth and Reconciliation Commission, but the actual number may be higher.*

Institutions and Institutional Racism

On page 20, Sam relates his experience of medical racism.

Are you aware of other episodes of this in Canada?

How do you think this can be addressed?

On page 25, Sam describes his father "signing our lives away." Later, he describes running away from St. Paul's School and being brought back in handcuffs.

What do you know about why parents complied with the government's requirement that children attend residential schools?

What is the implication or purpose of handcuffing children?

What would a child learn from being handcuffed?

Sam writes that before going to residential school, he didn't feel unsafe around white people. However, he later states that he learned to hate white people because of the abuse they (nuns, RCMP) perpetrated.

Can you see how these feelings would have an impact on Survivors' (including intergenerational Survivors) experiences in other institutions (e.g., college or university, workplace, hospital)?

Sam makes it clear that attendance at residential school had primed him for incarceration.

What are some of the factors described in this memoir that would lead to an overrepresentation of residential school Survivors in the justice system?

How do you think the same values that shaped residential school shaped, and continue to shape, law enforcement and the justice system?

Recovery and Return

When Sam attends rehab in Creston and then at Tsow-Tun Le Lum, he experiences the Sweat Lodge for the first time. While there, he writes down everything that had happened to him and feels relieved that it is finally outside of him.

Can you explain the significance of this, and why it helps Sam stay sober and get on a good path?

What do you understand about the importance for Survivors of telling their stories and being heard?

Sam describes the healing power of returning to his culture and watching the younger generation do the same. However, he also describes his skepticism about government programs and official reconciliation.

What would it look like for political and/or religious institutions to thoughtfully and concretely address the wrongs that they committed in a way that they might not have up to now?

Considering the schism between Sam's personal healing and his political skepticism, what in Sam's story still cries for justice?

What in Sam's story gives you hope?

The Ongoing Effects of Residential Schools

The Truth and Reconciliation Commission's final report, released in 2015, states:

> For over a century, the central goals of Canada's Aboriginal policy were to eliminate Aboriginal governments; ignore Aboriginal rights; terminate the Treaties; and, through a process of assimilation, cause Aboriginal

peoples to cease to exist as distinct legal, social, cultural, religious, and racial entities in Canada. The establishment and operation of residential schools were a central element of this policy, which can best be described as "cultural genocide." (Truth and Reconciliation Commission of Canada, 2015, *Honouring the Truth, Reconciling for the Future,* 1)

What does cultural genocide mean?

Knowing that unmarked graves are being found on the grounds of residential schools across Canada and that many children never made it home, do you believe that residential schools were an attempt at actual (and not just cultural) genocide? Explain how this is so.

Residential schools were founded on the idea that Indigenous people were inferior and needed to be assimilated.

Consider the institutions you are involved in: schools, churches or other religious institutions, hospitals, social service agencies, and so on.

In what ways do you think these institutions might mirror colonial values and/or be unwelcoming to Indigenous community members?

Many of the same policies and attitudes that led to the creation of residential schools also led to the Sixties Scoop and such things as birth alerts, resulting in Indigenous children being overrepresented in the foster care system to this day.

What are the similarities between the Sixties Scoop, birth alerts, and residential school? How do they continue to affect Indigenous communities?

RECONCILIATION/RECONCILIACTION

Educating yourself about the history of colonization and residential school is an important step on the road to reconciliation. The following are some suggestions for your own research and action:

- Find five Indigenous names of places near you. Learn what they mean and what their origin is.
- Learn what residential schools were open, and during what period, near where you live. Find out who ran them (e.g., the Anglican or Catholic Church) and if they were known for anything in particular.
- If you don't already know, learn the names of the Indigenous communities nearest you. What is/are their native language(s)? What traditions do they practise?
- Read up on the Indian Act as it exists today, to understand the way in which it still affects the lives of Indigenous people and communities.
- Learn about key moments of resistance in contemporary Indigenous history. You might look up the Oka Resistance, Ipperwash, the Marshall decision, the Delgamuukw decision, Idle No More, the Tsilhqot'in decision, the protests having to do with Wet'suwet'en Territory (see Unist'ot'en Camp), the anti-pipeline protests at Burnaby Mountain, and the anti-logging protests at Fairy Creek.
- If you haven't already, familiarize yourself with the Truth and Reconciliation Commission Calls to Action. Discuss them with friends and determine which ones are being acted on and which are not.

Finally, there's an abundance of contemporary Indigenous writers, filmmakers, musicians, dramatists, and visual and other artists on Turtle Island. Getting to know them is a great way to celebrate Indigenous culture today.

CRISIS SUPPORT

The following crisis support services are available 24/7.

Residential school survivors and family:
Indian Residential School Crisis Line, 1.866.925.4419

Individuals impacted by the issue of missing and murdered
Indigenous women, girls, and 2SLGBTQ+ people:
Missing and Murdered Indigenous Women and Girls
Crisis Line, 1.844.413.6649

First Nations, Inuit, and Métis peoples:
Hope for Wellness Helpline, 1.855.242.3310 or chat
online at hopeforwellness.ca

BC residents:
BC Mental Health Support Line 310.6789 (no area
code); province-wide Crisis Hotline, 1.800.784.2433

Canada Wide:
Talk Canada Suicide, 1.833.456.4566

ABOUT THE AUTHORS

Sam George (Sḵwx̱wú7mesh Úxwumixw/Squamish Nation) was born and raised on Eslhá7an (Mission Reserve) in North Vancouver and attended St. Paul's Indian Residential School for eight years. Following his school years, Sam worked as a longshoreman for forty-three years and served on Chief and Council for the Squamish Nation for twelve years. He has also been a drug and alcohol counsellor. Sam currently lives on Eslhá7an. He plays rhythm guitar (formerly organ) in a band called White Feather, which has been together for over fifty years.

Jill Yonit Goldberg teaches literature and creative writing at Langara College and has been involved in both curriculum development and teaching for Langara's Indigenous Upgrading program for students from xʷməθkʷəy̓əm Reserve No. 2. She lives with gratitude as an uninvited guest on the unceded, ancestral, and contemporary territories of the Sḵwx̱wú7mesh, xʷməθkʷəy̓əm, and Səl̓ílwətaʔ, and is a graduate of the University of British Columbia's MFA program in creative writing.

Liam Belson is honoured to be one of the students who worked on this project alongside Tanis Wilson and Dylan MacPhee.

Dylan MacPhee is a settler Canadian currently residing in Vancouver, BC, on the traditional unceded lands of the Sḵwx̱wú7mesh, xʷməθkʷəy̓əm, and Səl̓ílwətaʔ. Currently, Dylan is a fourth-year psychology student at the University of British Columbia, with plans to begin the counselling psychology master's program there in 2024. As a mature student, his change of career is motivated most prominently by his longing to give back to his community in a direct and meaningful way.

Tanis Wilson is an Indigenous Bachelor of Social Work student at Nicola Valley Institute of Technology. She is Omaškêko (Swampy Cree) from northern Ontario and a member of Constance Lake First Nation. She has been an uninvited guest on unceded xʷməθkʷəy̓əm, Sḵwx̱wú7mesh, and Səl̓ílwətaʔ territory for five years. A former Langara College student, Tanis enrolled in the Writing Lives course because she felt it aligned with the Truth and Reconciliation Commission Calls to Action related to education. Tanis also felt it would be an amazing opportunity to honour Indian residential school Survivors.

Printed and bound in Canada by Friesens

Set in Sero, Eames, and Baskerville
by Artegraphica Design Co.

Substantive editor: Lesley Erickson

Copy editor: Merrie-Ellen Wilcox

Proofreader: Alison Strobel

Cover designer: Jessica Sullivan